EASY PIANO

MAMMA MIA!

— HERE WE GO AGAIN —

THE MOVIE SOUNDTRACK FEATURING THE SONGS OF ABBA®

ISBN 978-1-5400-3321-5

Visit Hal Leonard Online at
www.halleonard.com

Contact Us:
Hal Leonard
7777 West Bluemound Road
Milwaukee, WI 53213
Email: info@halleonard.com

In Europe contact:
Hal Leonard Europe Limited
Distribution Centre, Newmarket Road
Bury St Edmunds, Suffolk, IP33 3YB
Email: info@halleonardeurope.com

In Australia contact:
Hal Leonard Australia Pty. Ltd.
4 Lentara Court
Cheltenham, Victoria, 3192 Australia
Email: info@halleonard.com.au

ANDANTE, ANDANTE

Words and Music by BENNY ANDERSSON
and BJÖRN ULVAEUS

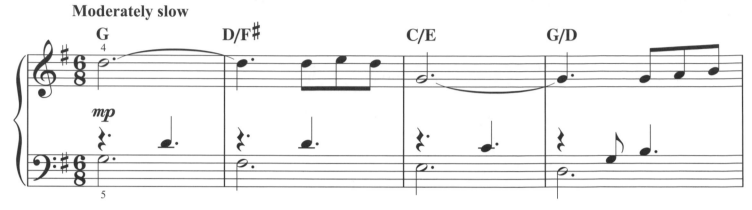

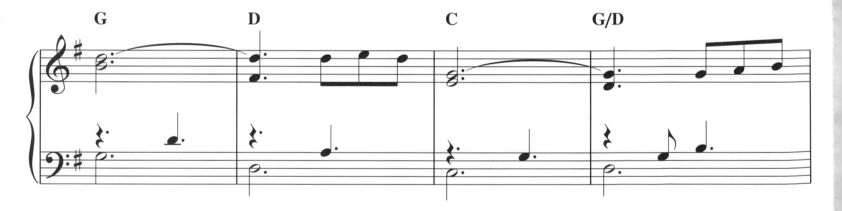

Take it

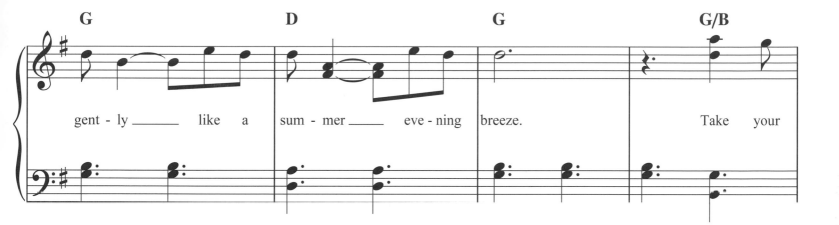

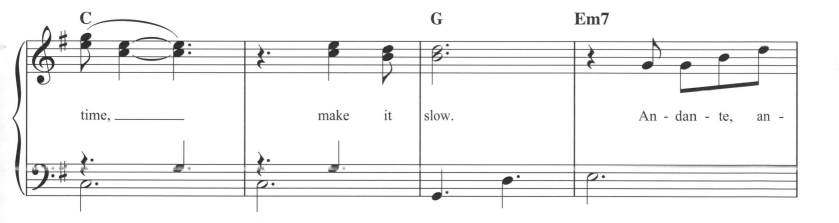

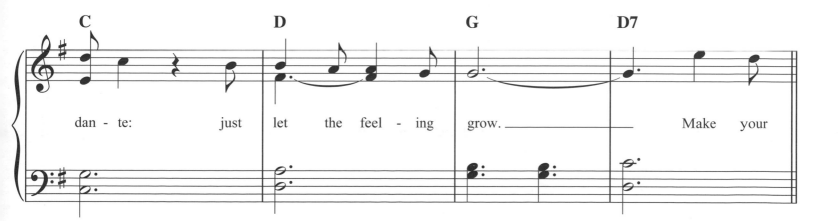

4

fin - gers _____ soft and light. Let your
shim - mer _____ in your eyes, like the

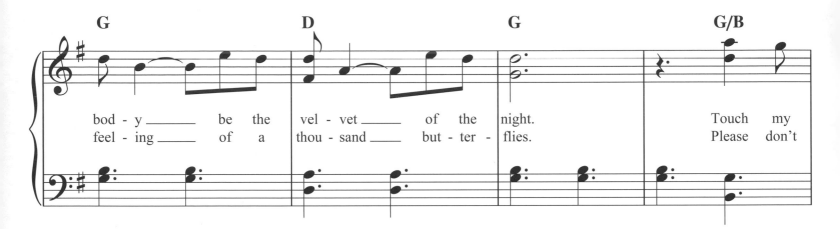

bod - y _____ be the vel - vet _____ of the night. Touch my
feel - ing _____ of a thou - sand _____ but - ter - flies. Please don't

soul, _____ you know how. An - dan - te, an -
talk; _____ go on, play, an - dan - te, an -

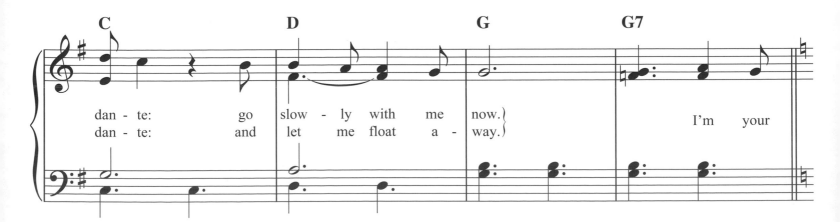

dan - te: go slow - ly with me now.⎫ I'm your
dan - te: and let me float a - way.⎭

mu - sic; _____ I'm your song. _____ Play me

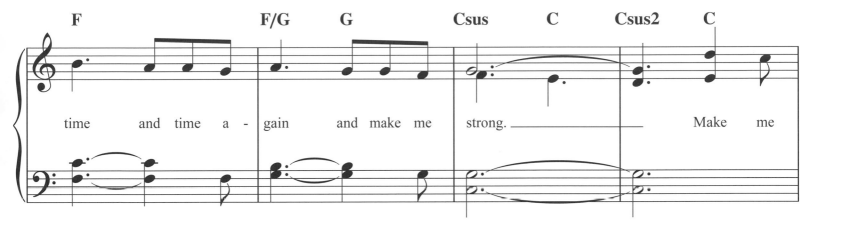

time and time a - gain and make me strong. _____ Make me

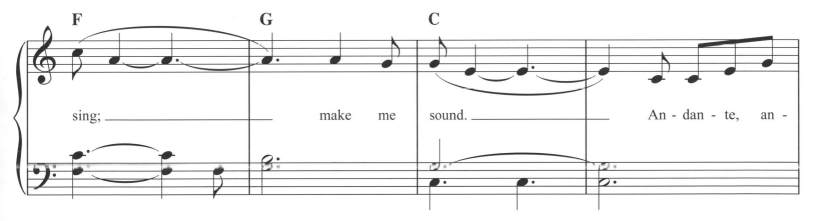

sing; _____ make me sound. _____ An - dan - te, an -

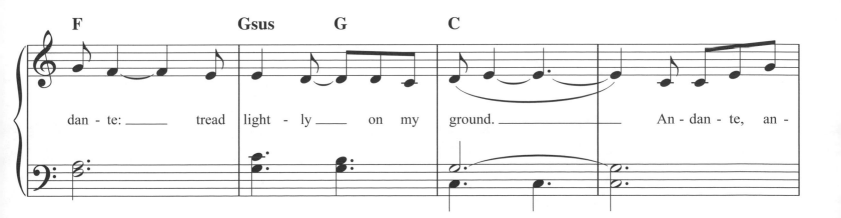

dan - te: _____ tread light - ly _____ on my ground. _____ An - dan - te, an -

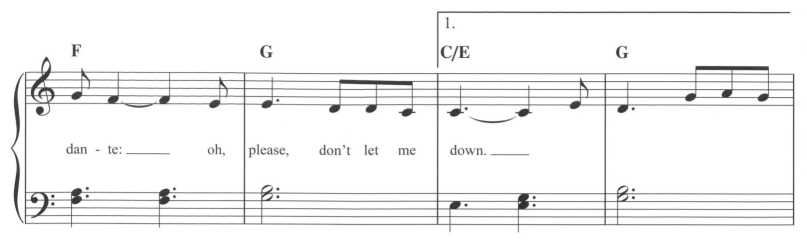

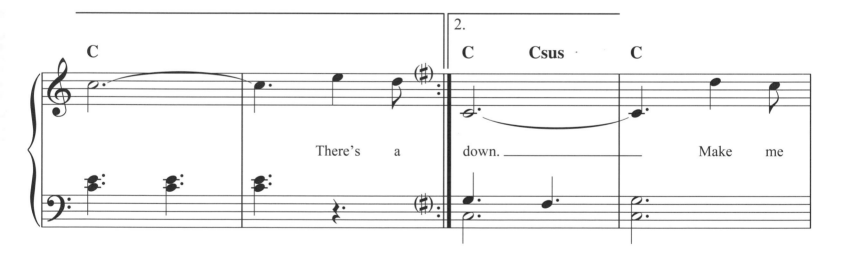

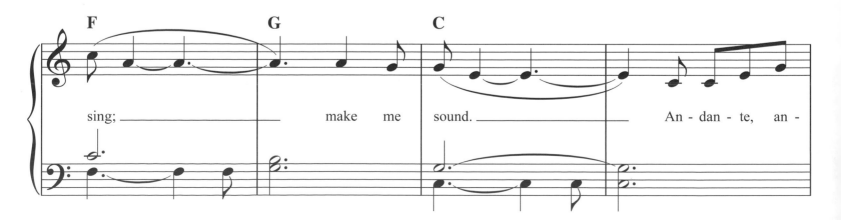

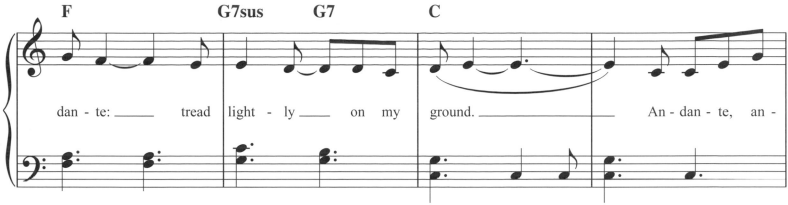

dan - te: _____ tread light - ly ____ on my ground. _____ An - dan - te, an -

dan - te: oh, please, don't let me ____

rit. *a tempo*

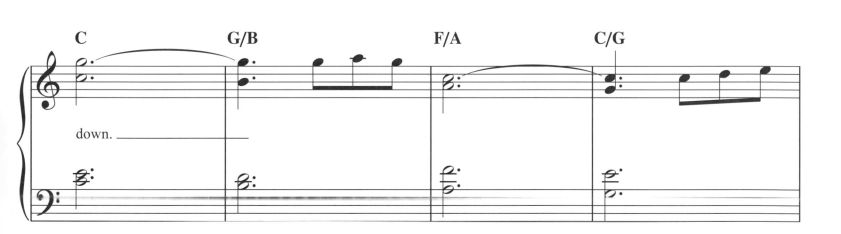

down. _____

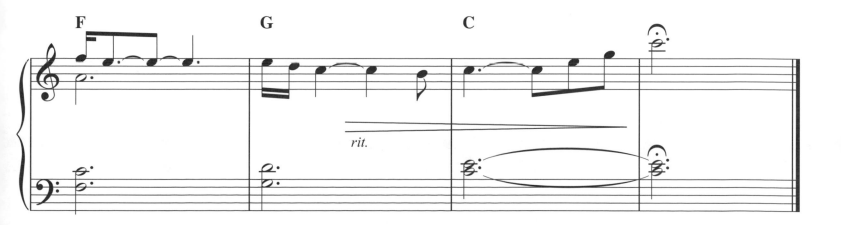

rit.

ANGEL EYES

Words and Music by BENNY ANDERSSON
and BJÖRN ULVAEUS

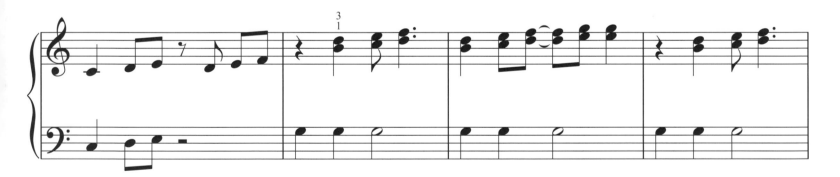

Last night   I was   tak - in' a walk a - long the
Some - times   when I'm   lone - ly I sit and think a -

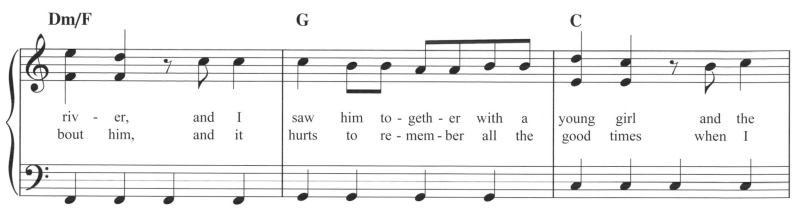

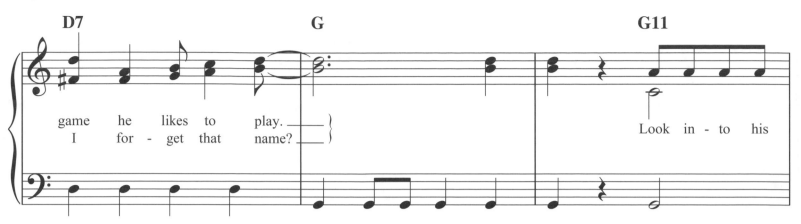

game he likes to play.
I for - get that name?

Look in - to his

an - gel eyes,
one look ___ and you're hyp - no - tized,

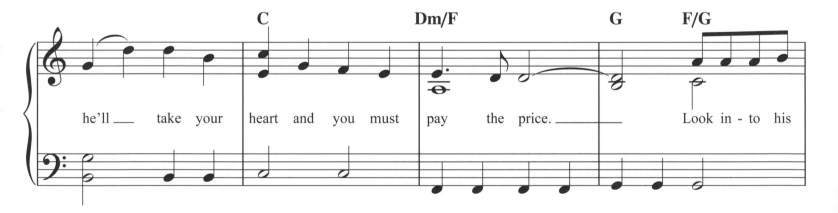

he'll ___ take your
heart and you must
pay the price. ___
Look in - to his

an - gel eyes,
you'll think ___ you're in
pa - ra - dise,

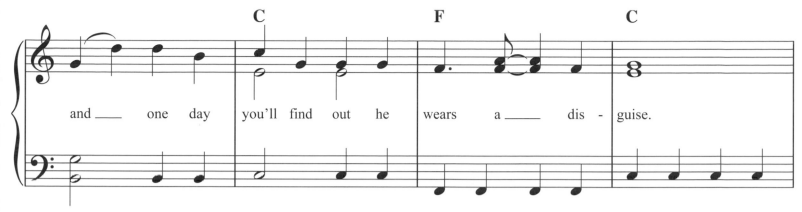

and ___ one day you'll find out he wears a ___ dis - guise.

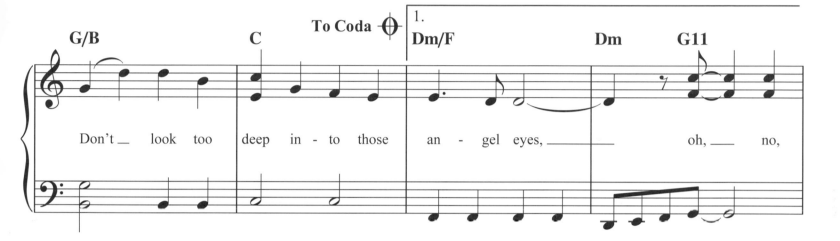

Don't ___ look too deep in - to those an - gel eyes, ___ oh, ___ no,

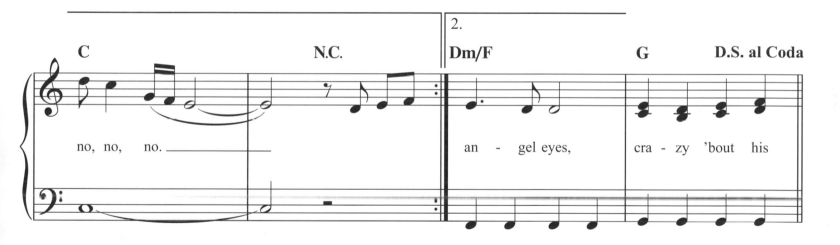

no, no, no. ___ an - gel eyes, cra - zy 'bout his

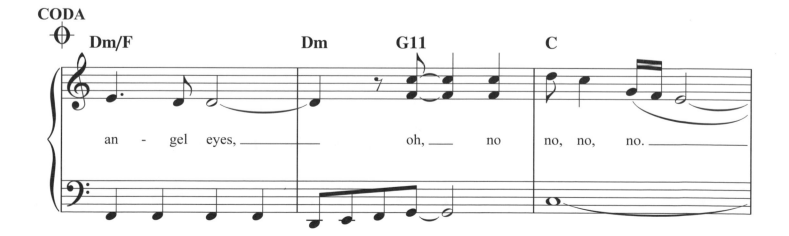

an - gel eyes, ___ oh, ___ no no, no, no. ___

N.C.

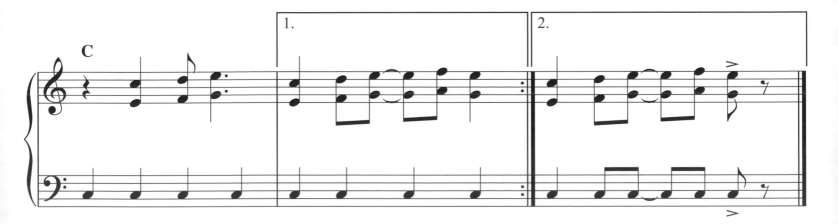

DANCING QUEEN

Words and Music by BENNY ANDERSSON,
BJÖRN ULVAEUS and STIG ANDERSON

Disco Rock

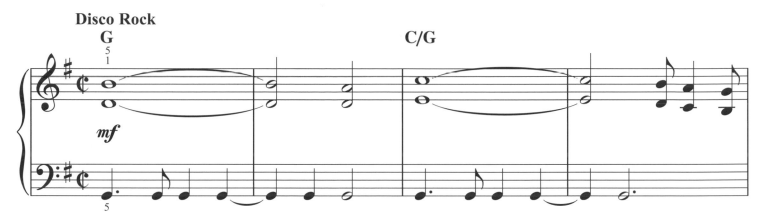

You __ can dance, __ you __ can jive, __

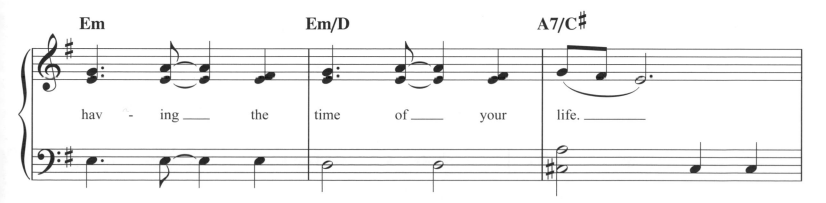

hav - ing __ the time of __ your life.

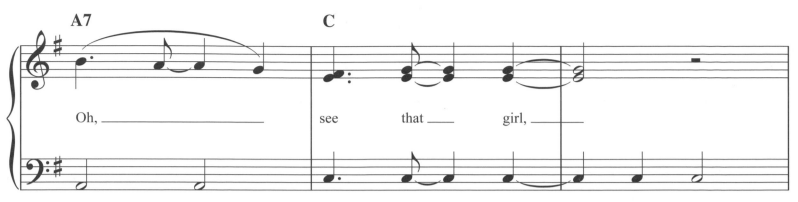

Oh, _____ see that ___ girl, _____

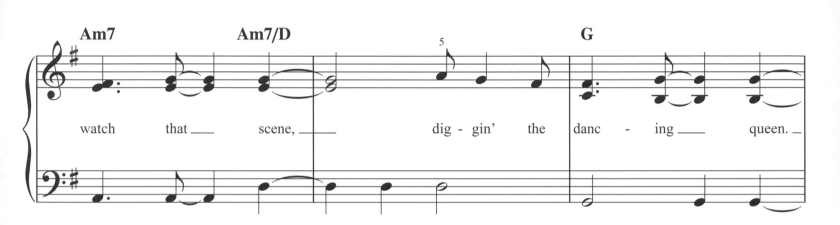

watch that ___ scene, _____ dig - gin' the danc - ing ___ queen. ___

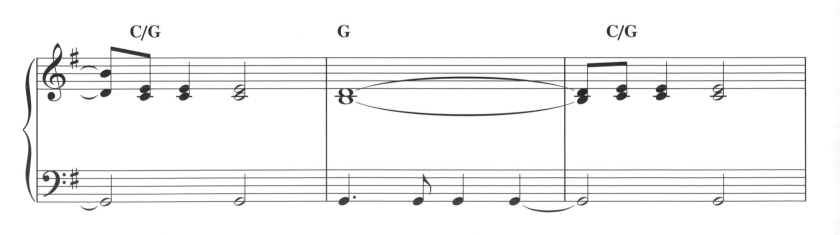

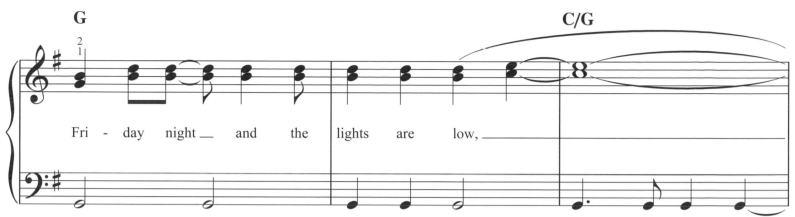

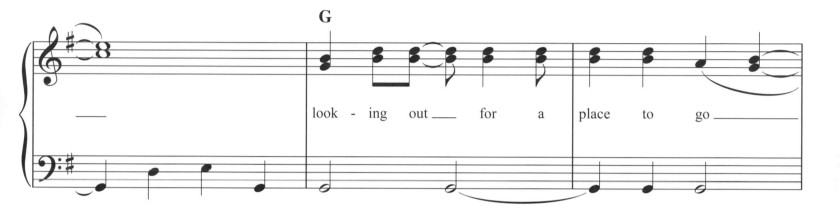

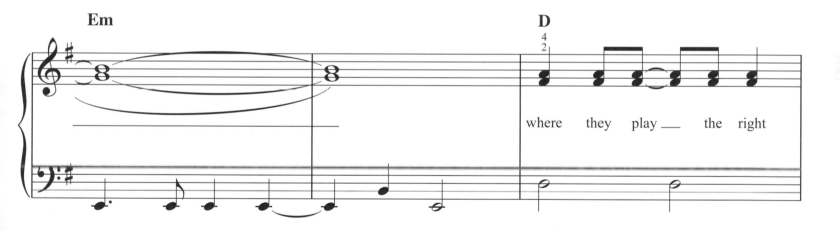

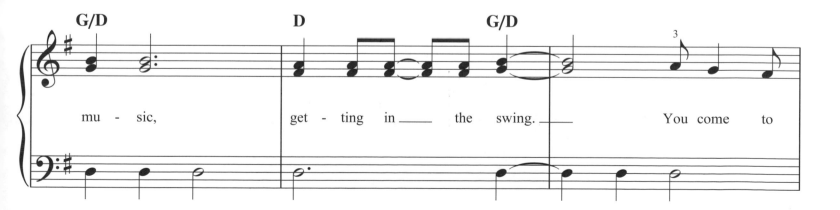

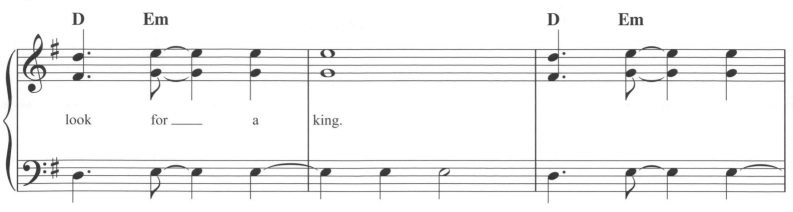

look for ___ a king.

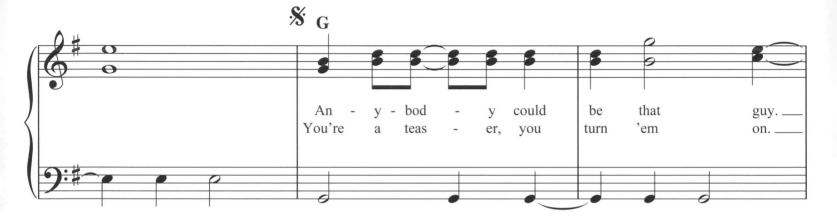

An - y - bod - y could be that guy. ___
You're a teas - er, you turn 'em on. ___

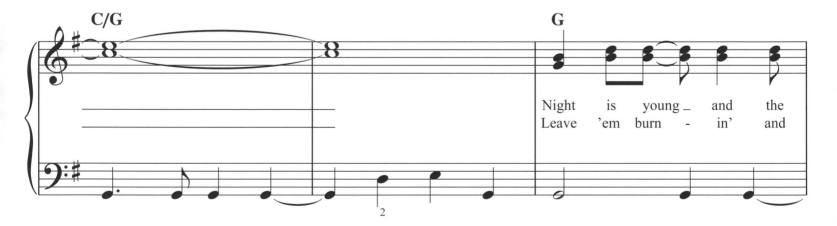

Night is young ___ and the
Leave 'em burn - in' and

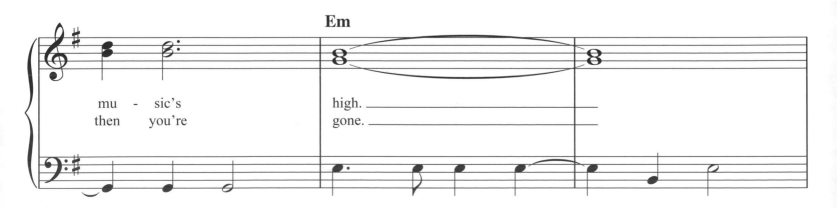

mu - sic's high. _____
then you're gone. _____

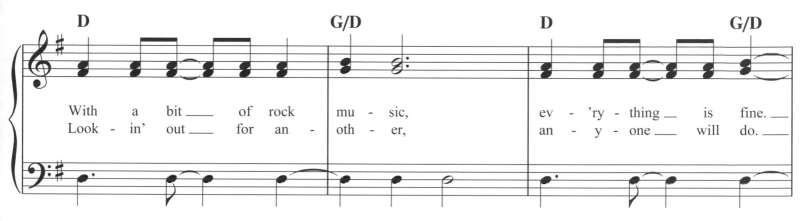

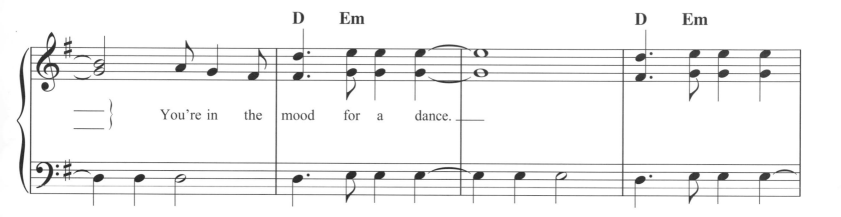

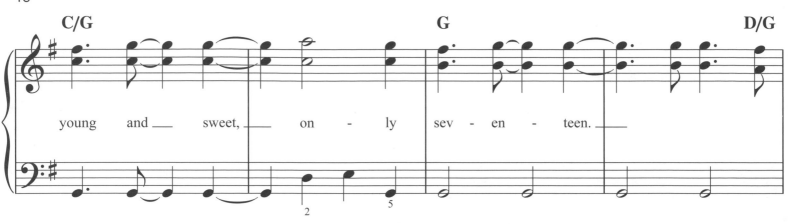

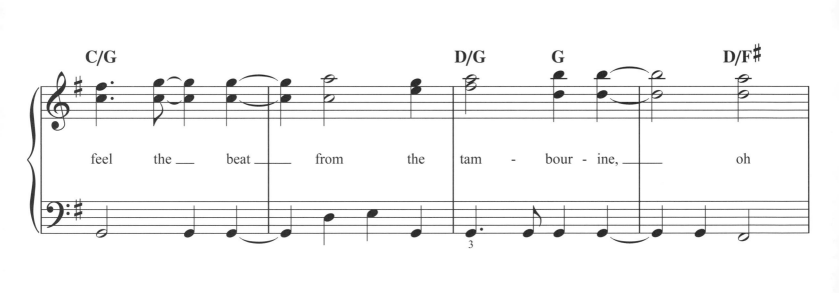

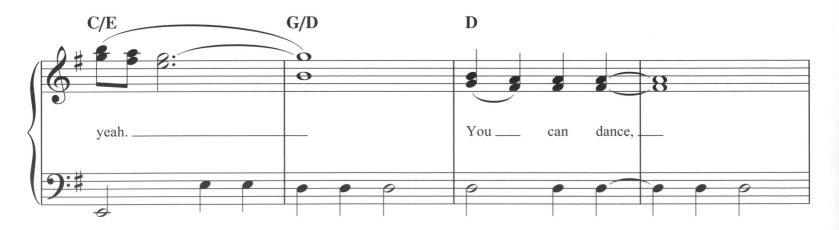

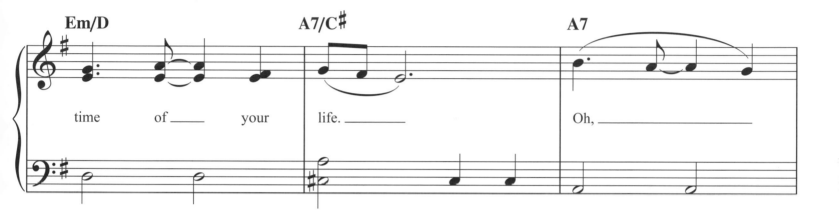

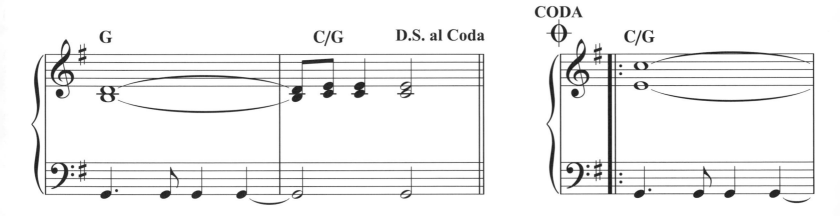

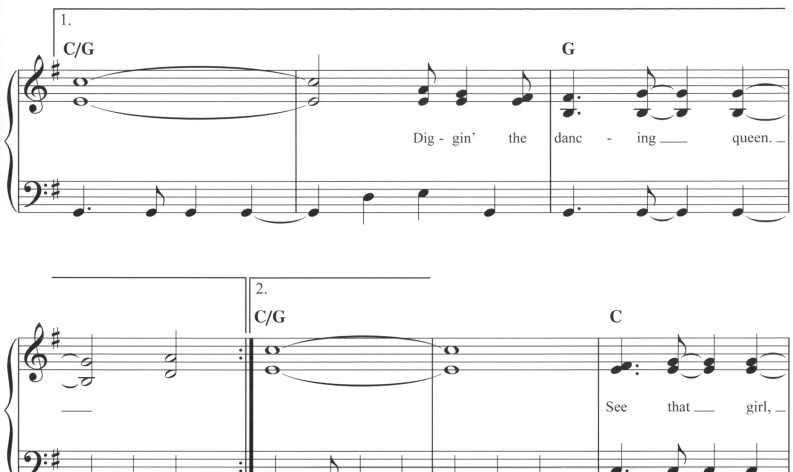

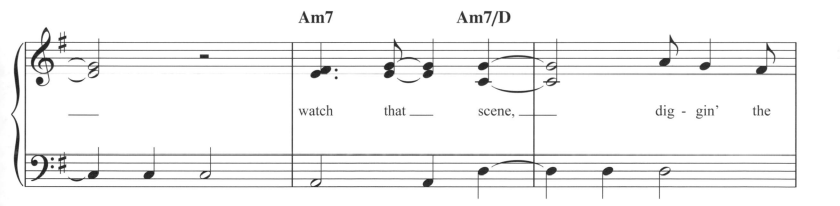

FERNANDO

Words and Music by BENNY ANDERSSON,
BJÖRN ULVAEUS and STIG ANDERSON

Moderately

Can you hear the drums, Fer - nan-do?
They were clos-er now, Fer - nan-do.
Now we're old and grey, Fer - nan-do.

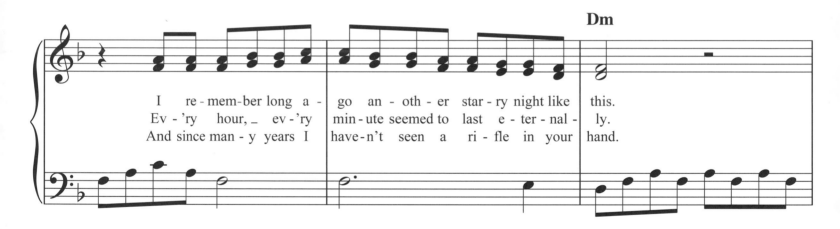

I re-mem-ber long a - go an-oth-er star-ry night like this.
Ev-'ry hour,_ ev-'ry min-ute seemed to last e-ter-nal - ly.
And since man-y years I have-n't seen a ri-fle in your hand.

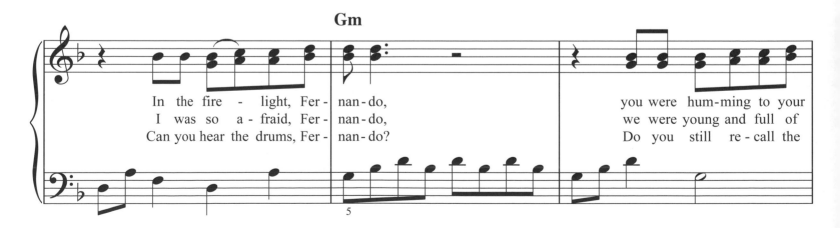

In the fire - light, Fer - nan-do,
I was so a - fraid, Fer - nan-do,
Can you hear the drums, Fer - nan-do?

you were hum-ming to your
we were young and full of
Do you still re-call the

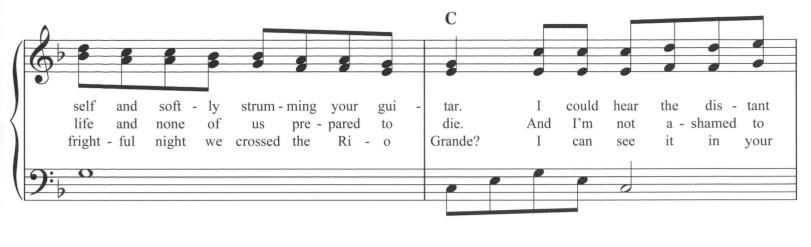

self and soft - ly strum - ming your gui - tar. I could hear the dis - tant
life and none of us pre - pared to die. And I'm not a - shamed to
fright - ful night we crossed the Ri - o Grande? I can see it in your

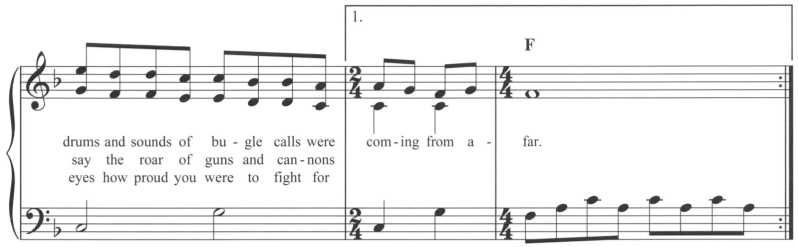

drums and sounds of bu - gle calls were com - ing from a - far.
say the roar of guns and can - nons
eyes how proud you were to fight for

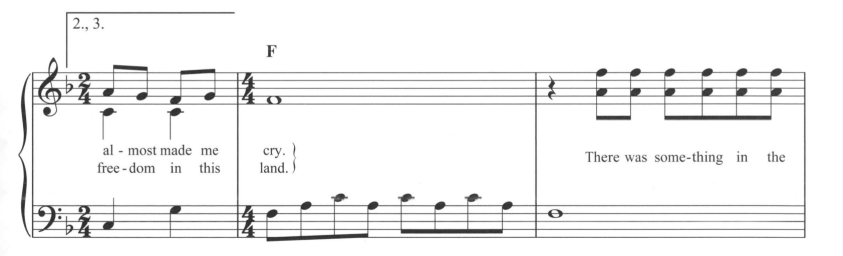

al - most made me cry.
free - dom in this land.

There was some - thing in the

air that night, _ the stars _ were bright, _ Fer - nan - do.

They were shin - ing there for you and me, ___ for lib - er - ty, ___ Fer - nan -

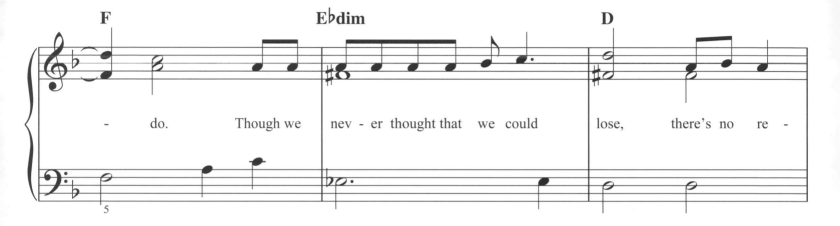

- do. Though we nev - er thought that we could lose, there's no re -

gret. ___ If I had to do the same a - gain, ___ I would, ___

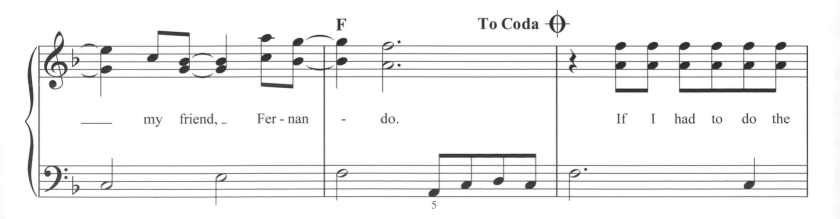

___ my friend, _ Fer - nan - do. If I had to do the

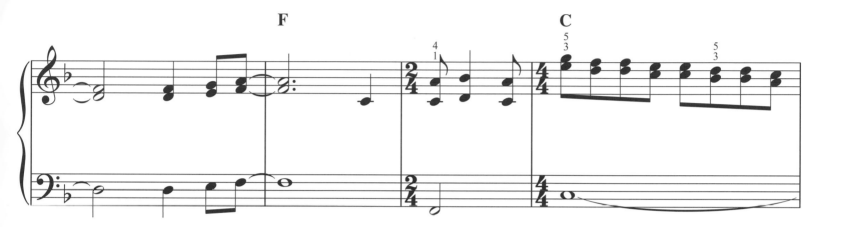

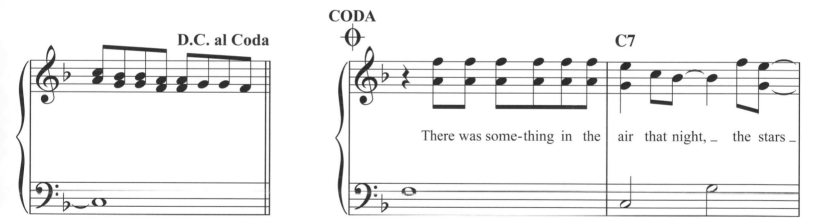

you and me, ___ for lib - er - ty, ___ Fer - nan - do. Though we

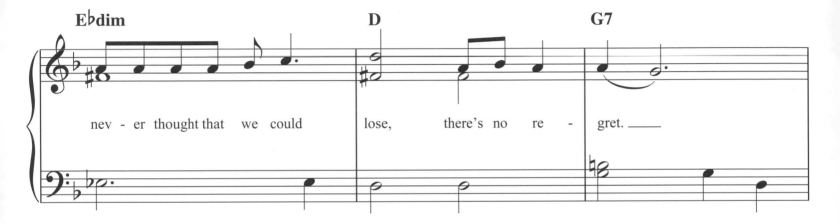

nev - er thought that we could lose, there's no re - gret. ___

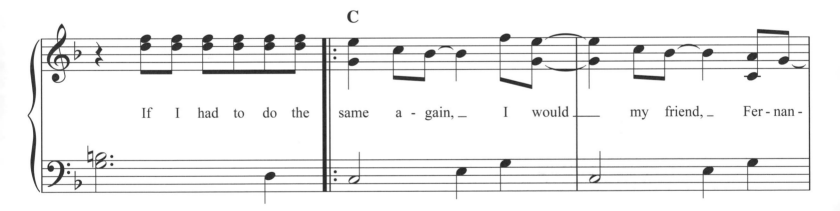

If I had to do the same a - gain, _ I would ___ my friend, _ Fer - nan -

- do.

If I had to do the

THE DAY BEFORE YOU CAME

Words and Music by BENNY ANDERSSON
and BJÖRN ULVAEUS

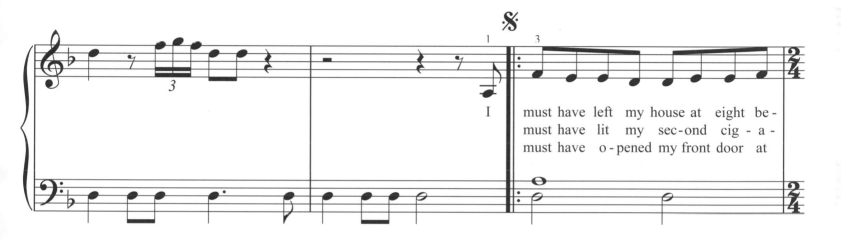

I
must have left my house at eight be-
must have lit my sec-ond cig-a-
must have o-pened my front door at

cause I al-ways   do.
rette at half-past   two.
eight o'-clock or   so,

My
And
and

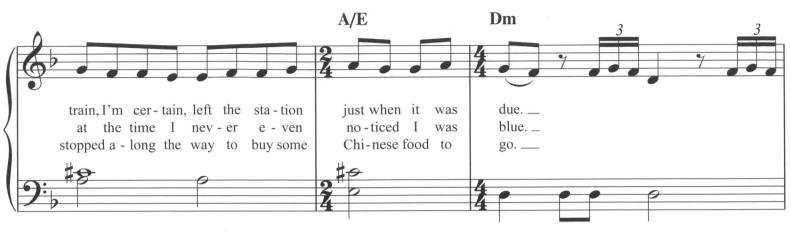

train, I'm cer - tain, left the sta - tion | just when it was | due. ___
at the time I nev - er e - ven | no - ticed I was | blue. ___
stopped a - long the way to buy some | Chi - nese food to | go. ___

I | must have read the morn - ing pa - pers, | go - ing in - to
I | must have kept on drag - ging through the | busi - ness of the
I'm | sure I had my din - ner watch - ing | some - thing on T.

town | | and | hav - ing got - ten through the e - di -
day | | and | with - out real - ly know - ing an - y -
V. | | There's | not a sin - gle ep - i - sode of

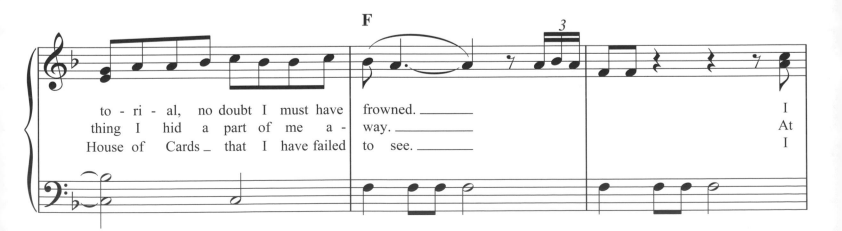

to - ri - al, no doubt I must have | frowned. ___ | I
thing I hid a part of me a - | way. ___ | At
House of Cards __ that I have failed | to see. ___ | I

must have made my desk
six   I   must have left,
must have gone to bed

a - round   a   quar - ter   af - ter   nine, _____
there's no ex - cep - tion to the   rule. _____
a - round   a   quar - ter   af - ter   ten. _____

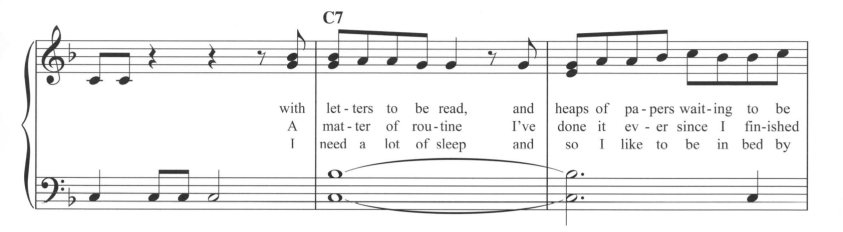

with   let - ters   to   be   read,   and   heaps of pa-pers wait-ing to be
A   mat - ter   of   rou - tine   I've   done it ev - er since I fin-ished
I   need   a   lot   of   sleep   and   so   I like to be in bed by

signed. _____
school. _____
then. _____

I
The
I

must have gone to lunch   at
train back home a - gain,   un -
must have read   a while   the

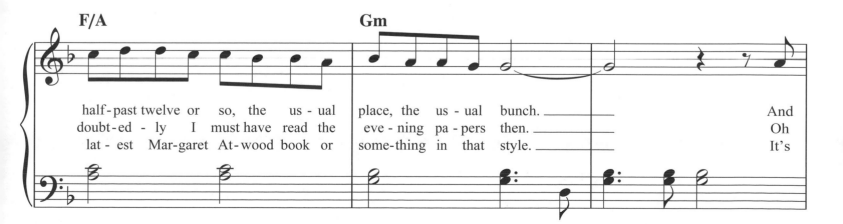

half - past twelve or   so, the us - ual
doubt - ed - ly   I   must have read the
lat - est Mar-garet At - wood book or

place, the us - ual bunch. _____
eve - ning pa - pers   then. _____
some-thing in that style. _____

And
Oh
It's

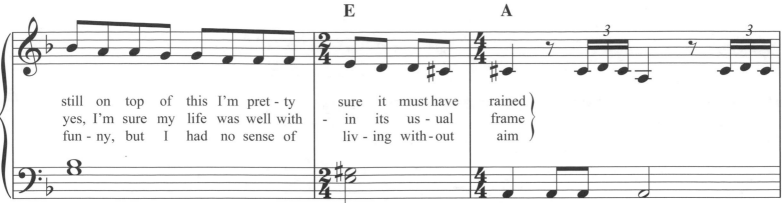

still on top of this I'm pret - ty
yes, I'm sure my life was well with
fun - ny, but I had no sense of

sure it must have
- in its us - ual
liv - ing with - out

rained
frame
aim

the day be - fore you came. _____

I

came.

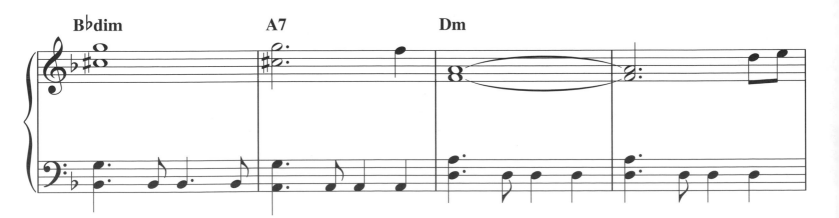

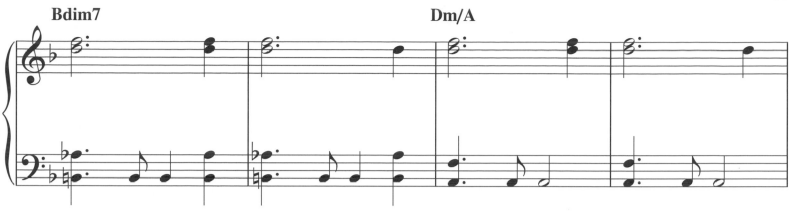

Bdim7   **Dm/A**

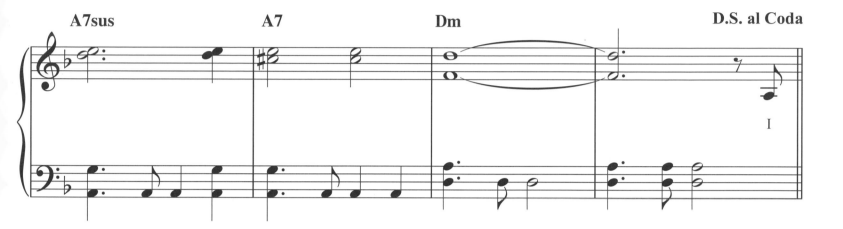

A7sus   **A7**   **Dm**   **D.S. al Coda**

I

CODA

Dm   **B♭**

came.   And   turn - ing   out   the   light   I

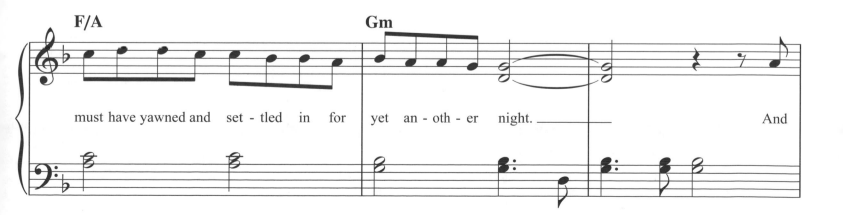

F/A   **Gm**

must have yawned and   set - tled   in   for   yet   an - oth - er   night.   And

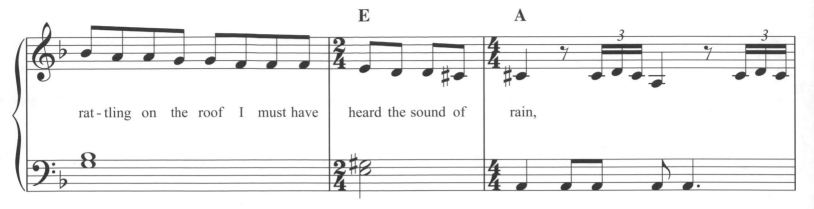

rat-tling on the roof I must have | heard the sound of | rain,

the day be-fore you came.

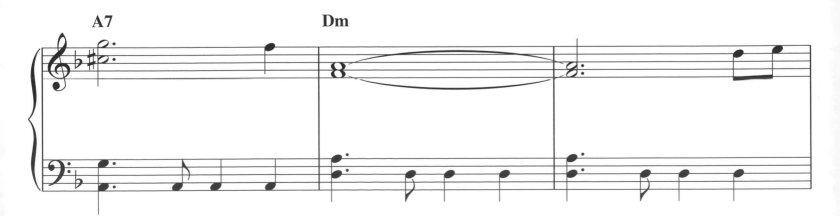

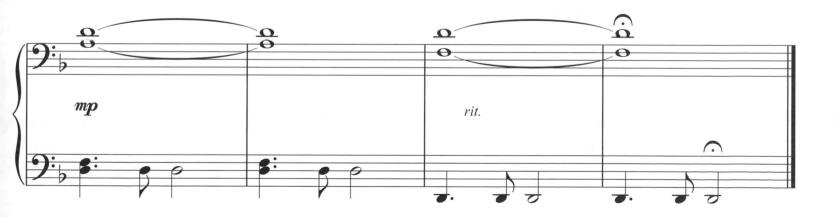

I HAVE A DREAM

Words and Music by BENNY ANDERSSON
and BJÖRN ULVAEUS

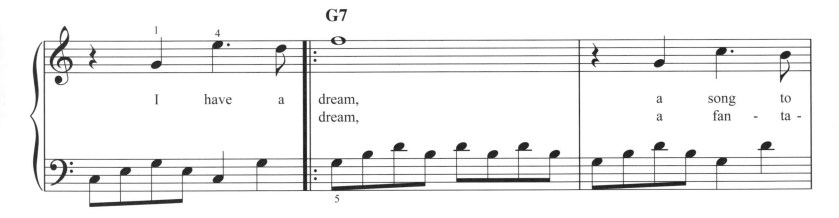

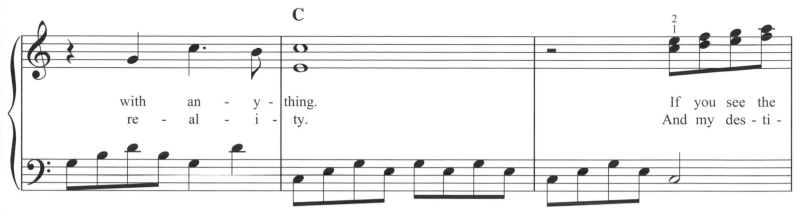

with an - y - thing.
re - al - i - ty.

If you see the
And my des - ti -

won - der
na - tion

of a fair - y - tale,
makes it worth the while,

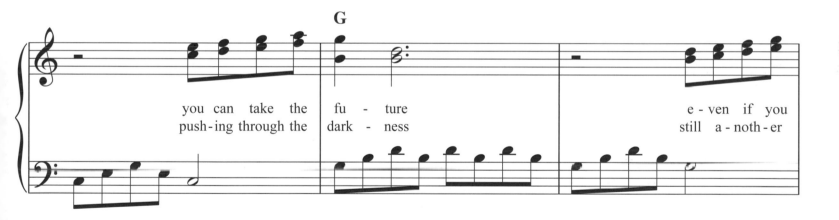

you can take the
push - ing through the

fu - ture
dark - ness

e - ven if you
still a - noth - er

fail.
mile.

To Coda

I be - lieve in an - gels,

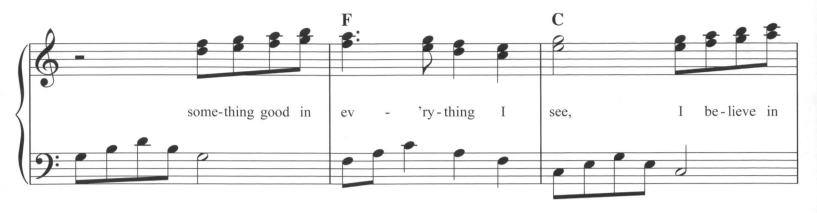

some-thing good in ev - 'ry-thing I see, I be-lieve in

an - gels. When I know the time is right for

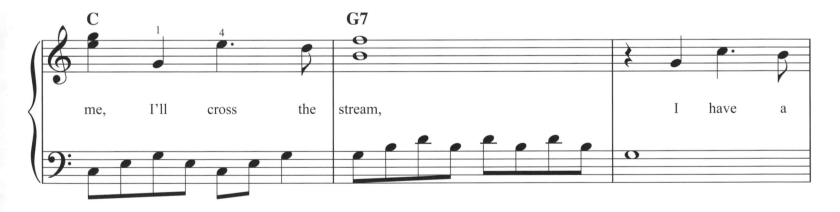

me, I'll cross the stream, I have a

dream. I have a dream,

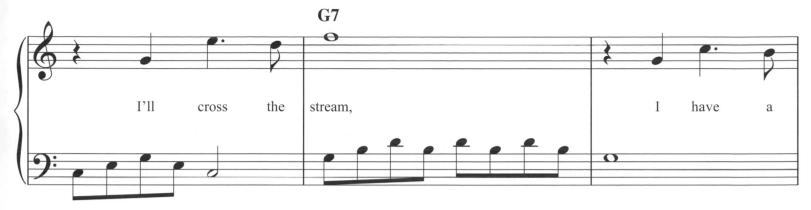

I'll cross the stream, I have a

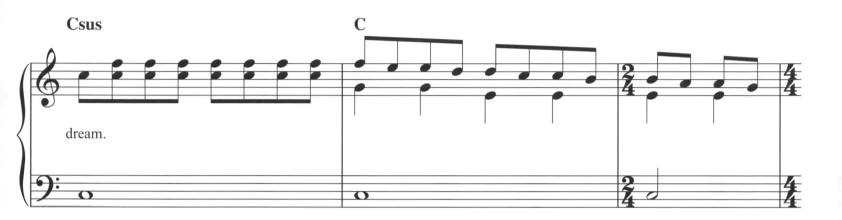

dream.

I be-lieve

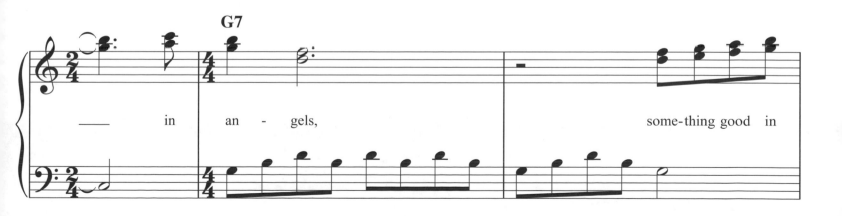

in an - gels, some-thing good in

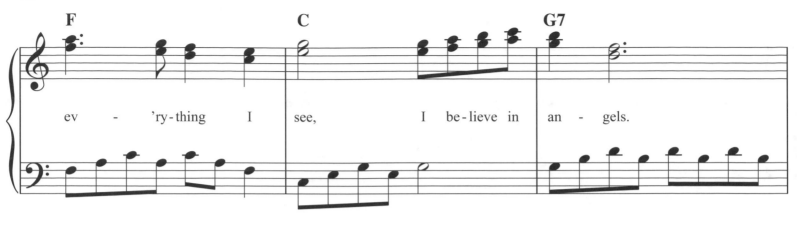

ev - 'ry-thing I see, I be - lieve in an - gels.

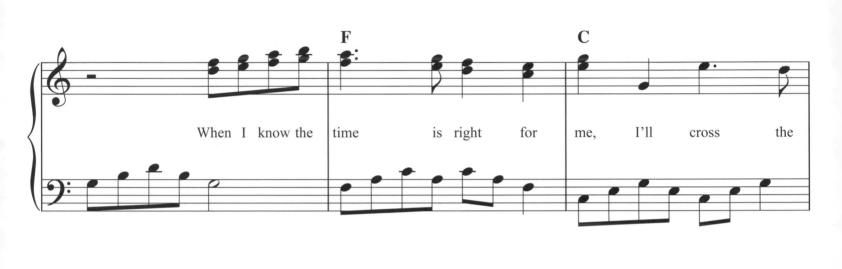

When I know the time is right for me, I'll cross the

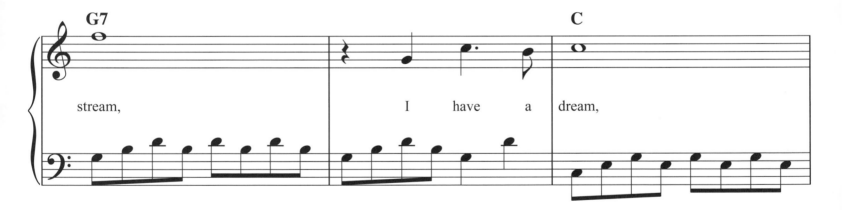

stream, I have a dream,

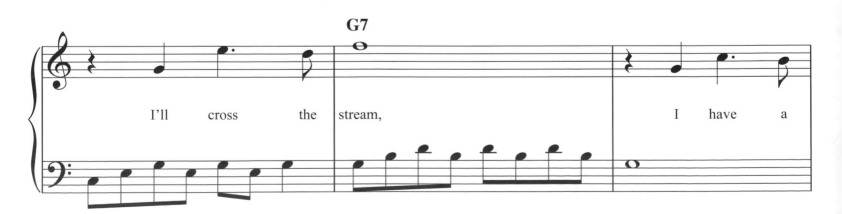

I'll cross the stream, I have a

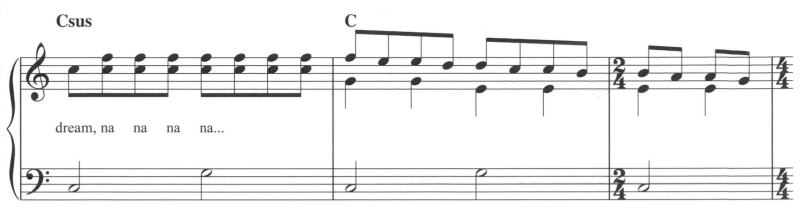

dream, na   na   na   na...

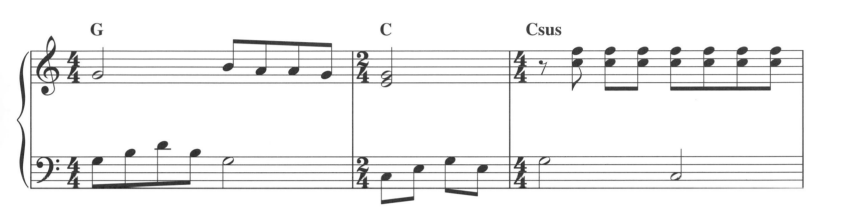

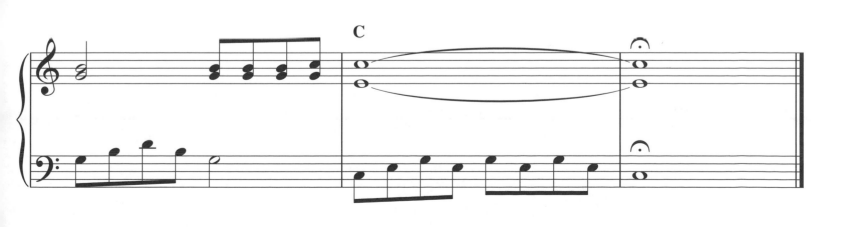

I WONDER (DEPARTURE)

Words and Music by BENNY ANDERSSON,
BJÖRN ULVAEUS and STIG ANDERSON

Moderately slow

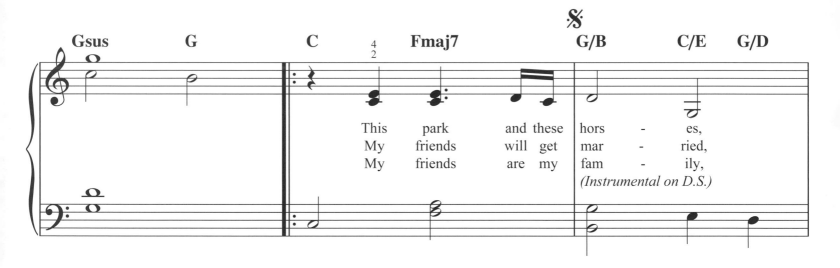

This park and these hors - es,
My friends will get mar - ried,
My friends are my fam - ily,
(Instrumental on D.S.)

old streets I have walked,
have chil - dren and homes,
this cit - y I love,

ev - 'ry-thing dear, ___
it sounds so nice, ___
bu - ses I've missed, ___

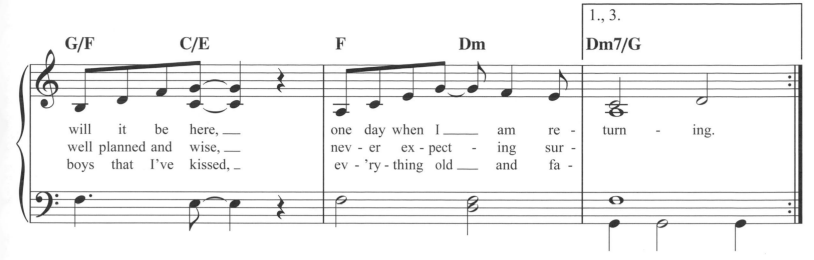

G/F   **C/E**   **F**   **Dm**   **1., 3.**   **Dm7/G**

will it be here, ___ one day when I ___ am re - turn - ing.
well planned and wise, ___ nev - er ex - pect - ing sur -
boys that I've kissed, ___ ev - 'ry - thing old ___ and fa -

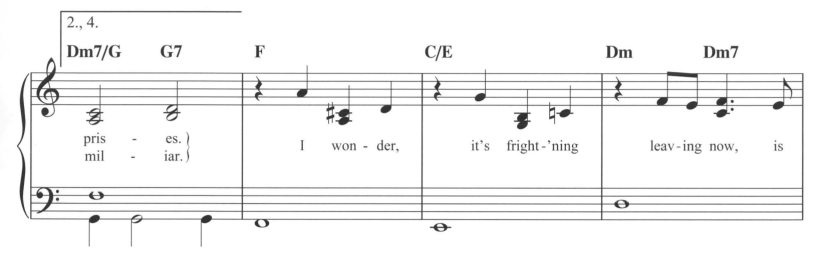

2., 4.   **Dm7/G**   **G7**   **F**   **C/E**   **Dm**   **Dm7**

pris - es. ⎱
mil - iar. ⎰   I won - der, it's fright -'ning leav - ing now, is

Gm7   **Gm7/C C**   **F**   **G/F**   **Em**   **Am7**   **Dm9**   **E7**   **Am**

that the right thing? I won - der, it scares me, but who the hell ___ am I

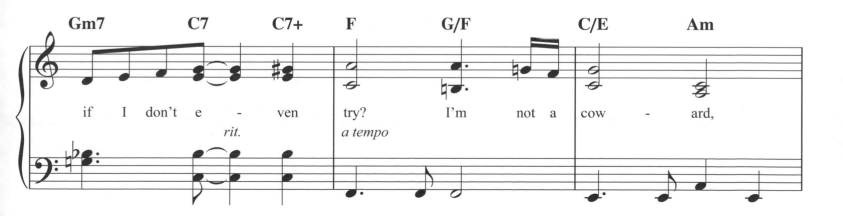

Gm7   **C7**   **C7+**   **F**   **G/F**   **C/E**   **Am**

if I don't e - ven try? I'm not a cow - ard,
              rit.   *a tempo*

KISSES OF FIRE

Words and Music by BENNY ANDERSSON
and BJÖRN ULVAEUS

With motion, rubato

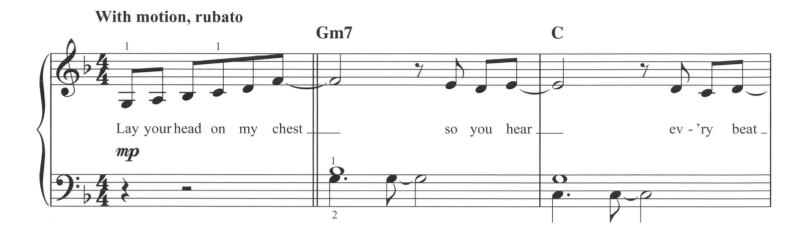

Lay your head on my chest ___ so you hear ___ ev-'ry beat ___

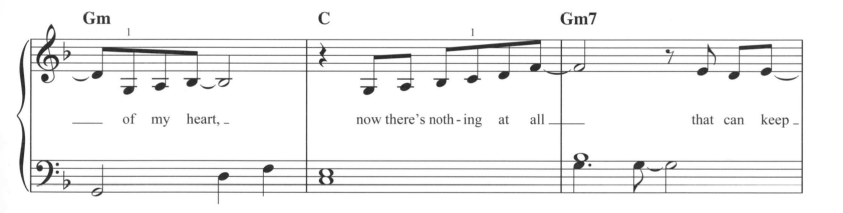

___ of my heart, ___ now there's noth-ing at all ___ that can keep ___

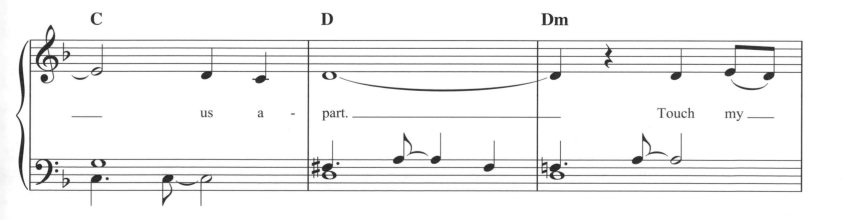

___ us a - part. ___ Touch my ___

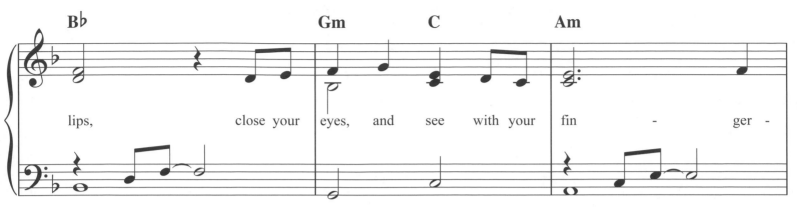

lips,　　　　close your eyes,　and　see with your fin - ger -

tips　　　things　　that you do,　　　and you

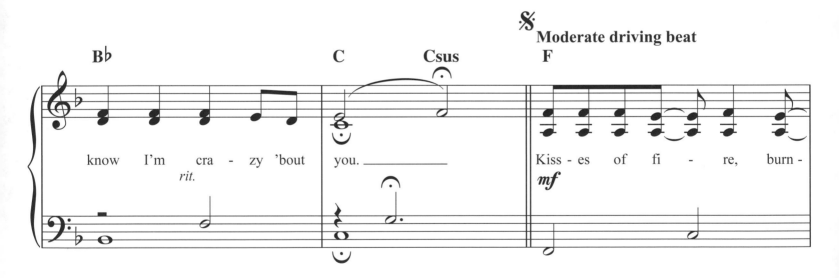

know I'm cra - zy 'bout you. ___ Kiss - es of fi - re, burn -

Moderate driving beat

rit.

mf

- ing, burn - ing,　I'm at the point _ of no ___ re - turn - ing.

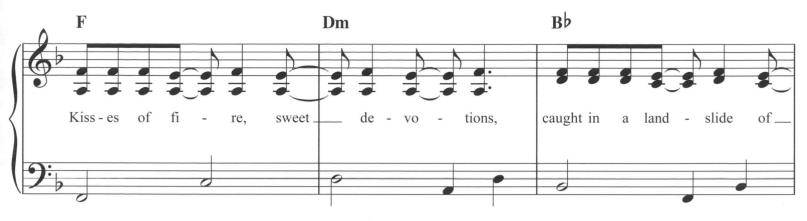

Kiss - es of fi - re, sweet __ de - vo - tions, caught in a land - slide of __

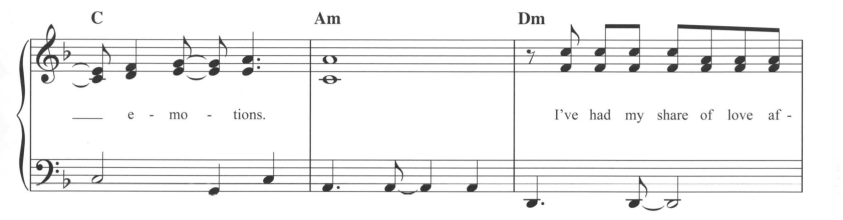

__ e - mo - tions. I've had my share of love af -

fairs, and they were noth - ing com - pared __ to this. Ah,

I'm rid - ing high - er than the sky, and there is fi - re in ev - 'ry kiss.

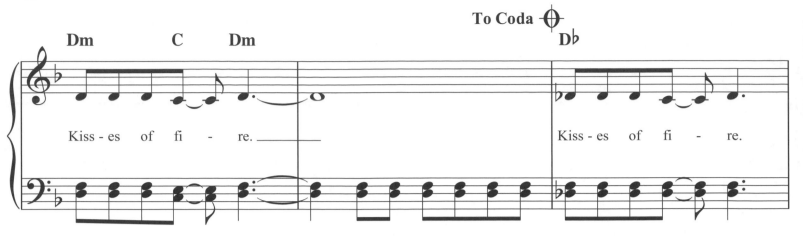

To Coda

Kiss - es of fi - re. _____ Kiss - es of fi - re.

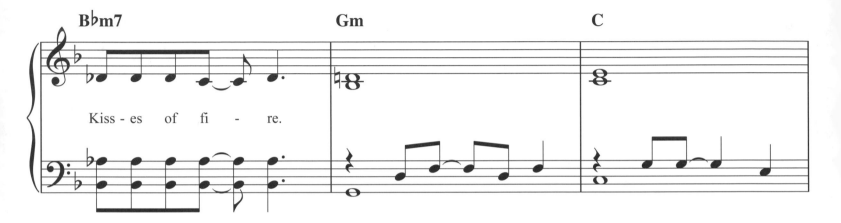

Kiss - es of fi - re.

When you sleep by my side _____ I feel safe _

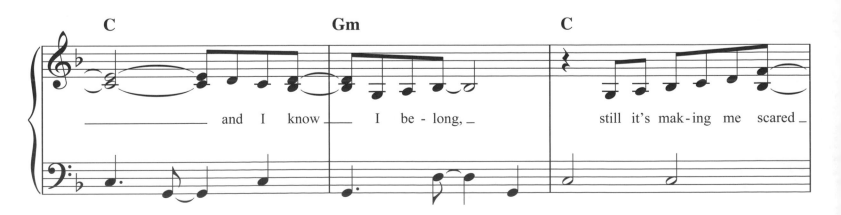

_____ and I know _ I be - long, _ still it's mak - ing me scared _

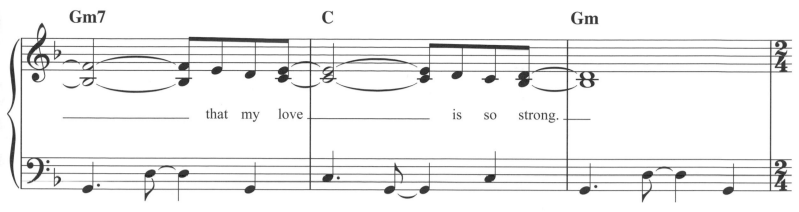

CODA

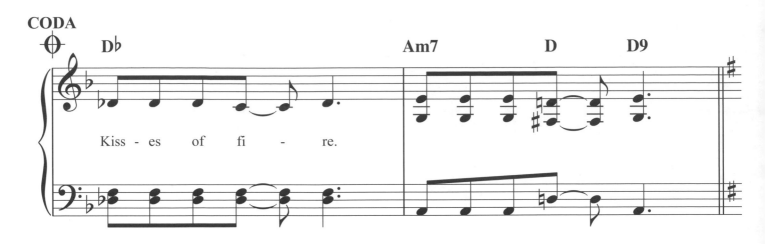

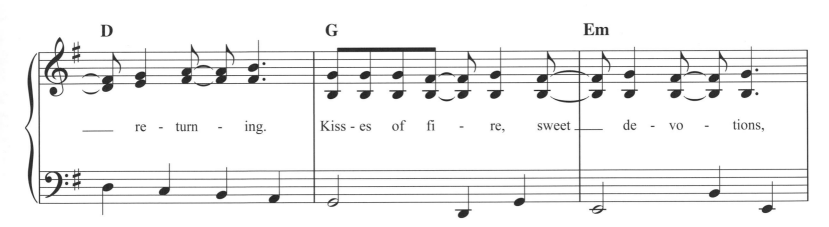

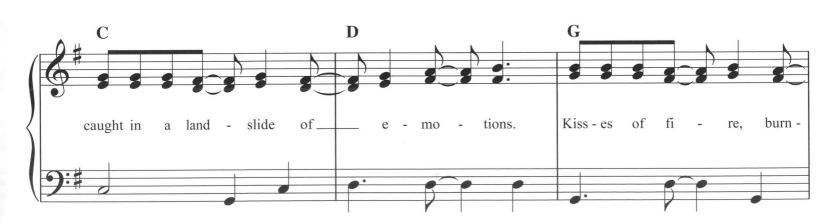

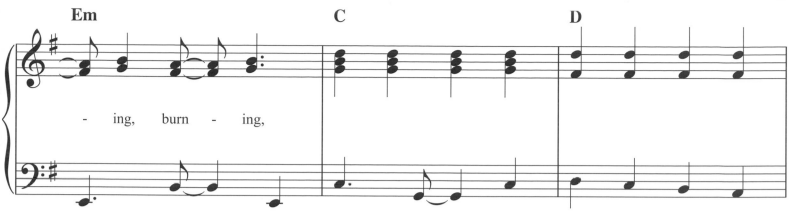

- ing, burn - ing,

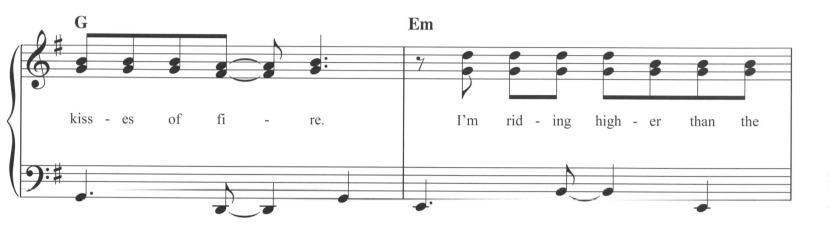

kiss - es of fi - re. I'm rid - ing high - er than the

sky, and there is fi - re in ev - 'ry kiss.

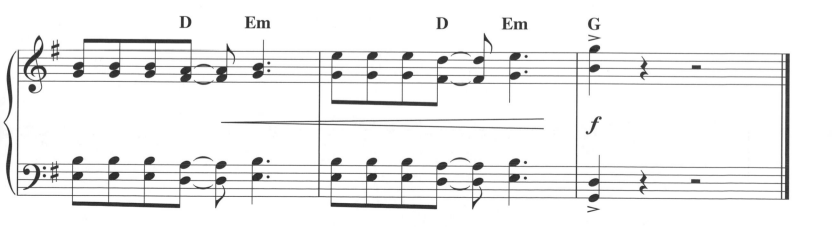

I'VE BEEN WAITING FOR YOU

Words and Music by BENNY ANDERSSON
and BJÖRN ULVAEUS

Moderately slow

I, I have known love be - fore; I thought it would no

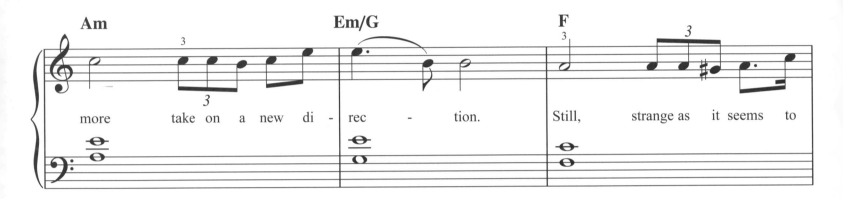

more take on a new di - rec - tion. Still, strange as it seems to

be, it's tru - ly new to me, that af - fec - tion. *poco rall.*

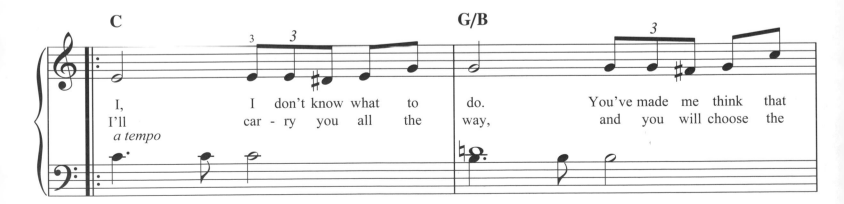

I, I don't know what to do. You've made me think that

I'll car - ry you all the way, and you will choose the

a tempo

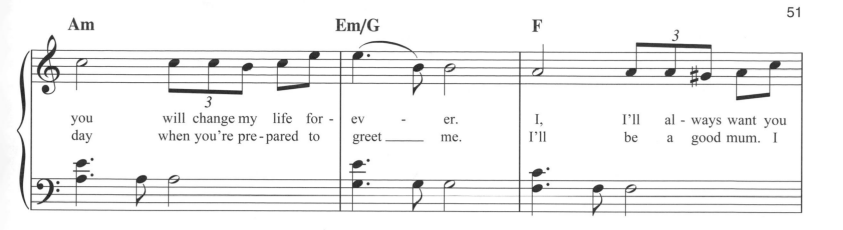

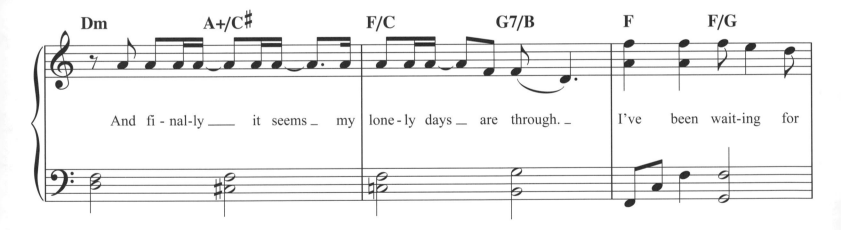

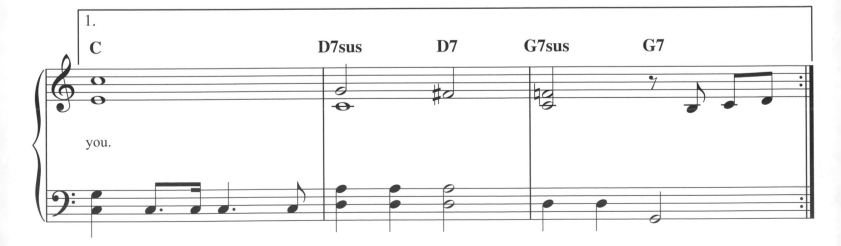

you. Oh,_____ I've been wait - ing for

you. Na na na, na na na, na na___ na.

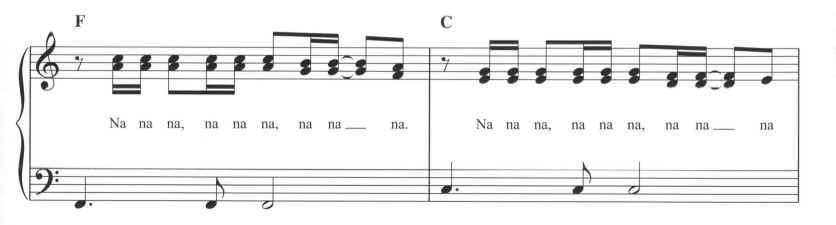

Na na na, na na na, na na___ na. Na na na, na na na, na na___ na

na. na. *rit.*

KNOWING ME, KNOWING YOU

Words and Music by BENNY ANDERSSON,
BJÖRN ULVAEUS and STIG ANDERSON

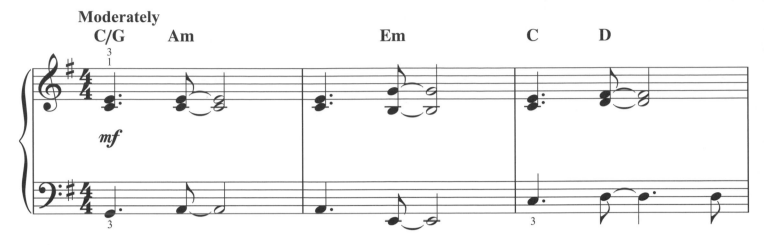

No more — care - free — laugh - ter, —
Mem - 'ries, — good days, — bad days. —

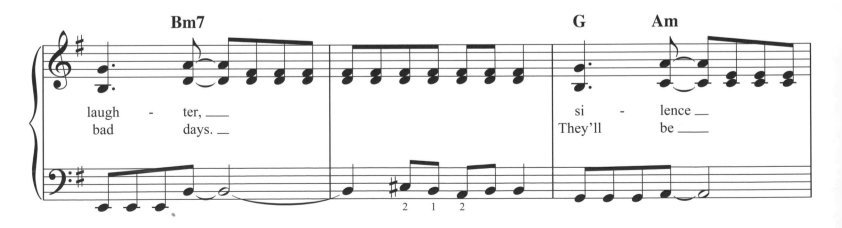

si - lence —
They'll be —

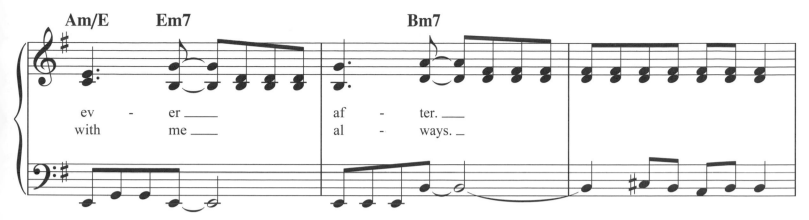

ev - er ____ af - - ter. ____
with me ____ al - ways. ____

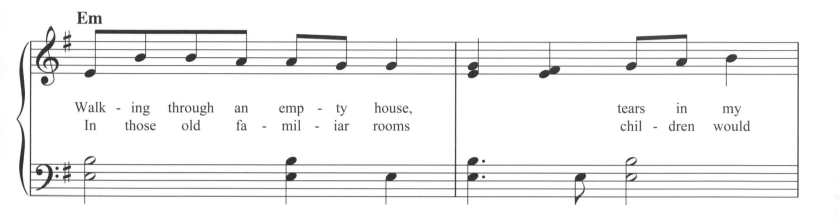

Walk - ing through an emp - ty house,   tears in my
In those old fa - mil - iar rooms   chil - dren would

eyes.   Here is where the sto - ry ends, ___
play.   Now there's on - ly emp - ti - ness, ___

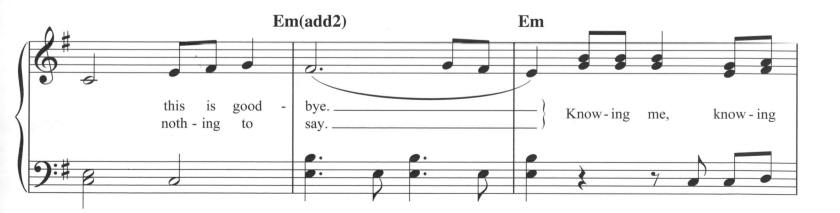

this is good - bye. ____   Know - ing me, know - ing
noth - ing to say. ____

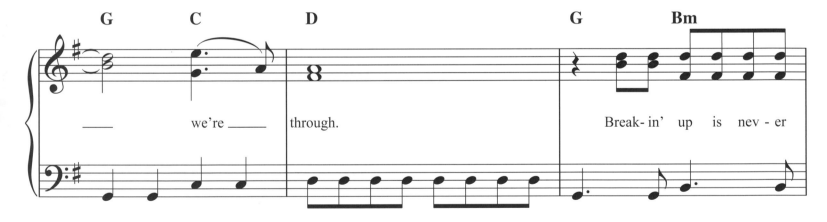

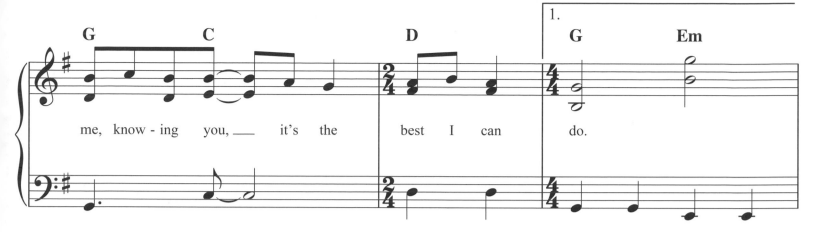

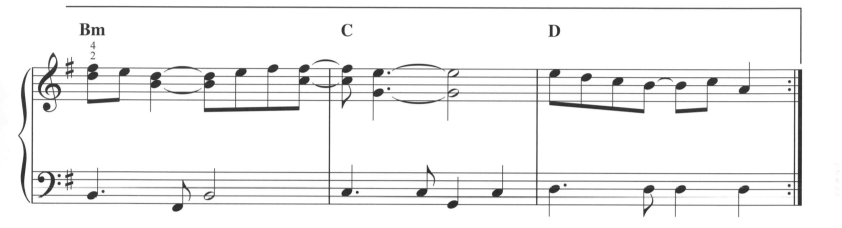

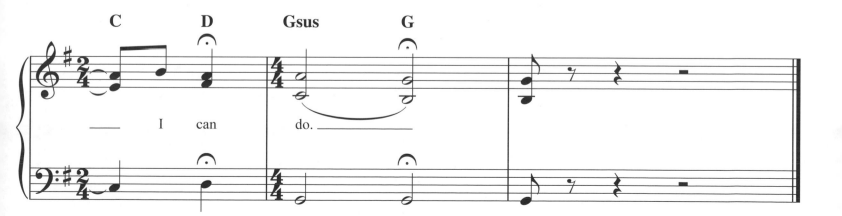

MAMMA MIA

Words and Music by BENNY ANDERSSON,
BJÖRN ULVAEUS and STIG ANDERSON

I was cheat-ed by you
I was an-gry and sad

and I think you know when.
a-bout things that you do.

So I made up my mind it must come to an
I can't count all the times that I've cried o-ver

end.
you.

Look at me now, ___
And when you go, ___

will I ev - er learn?
when you slam the door,

I don't know how, ___
I think you know ___

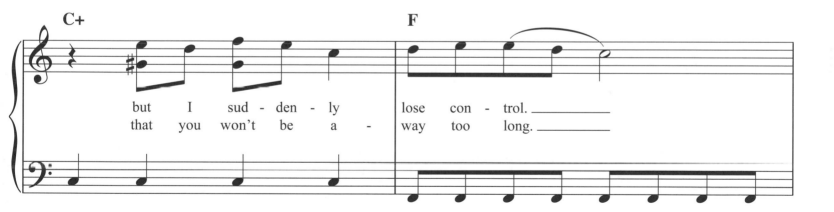

but I sud - den - ly
that you won't be a -

lose con - trol. ___
way too long. ___

There's a fire ___ with - in my soul. ___
You know ___ that I'm not that strong. ___

Just one

60

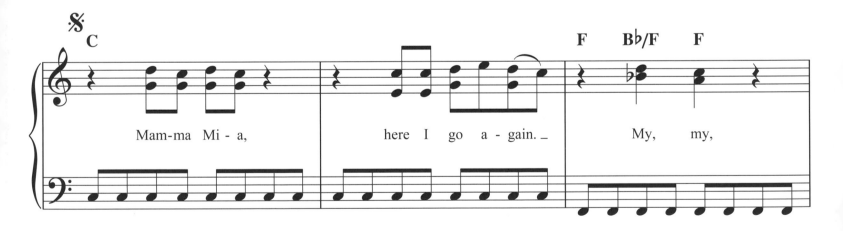

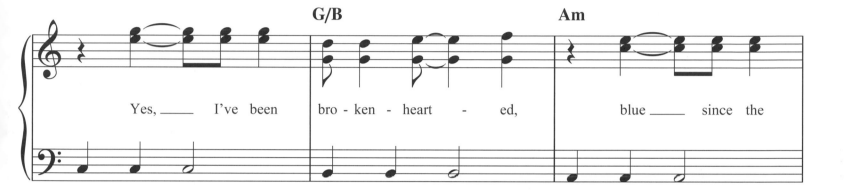

1.

Dm7　　　　G　　　　　　C　　　　　　　　C+

I should not have let you go. ___

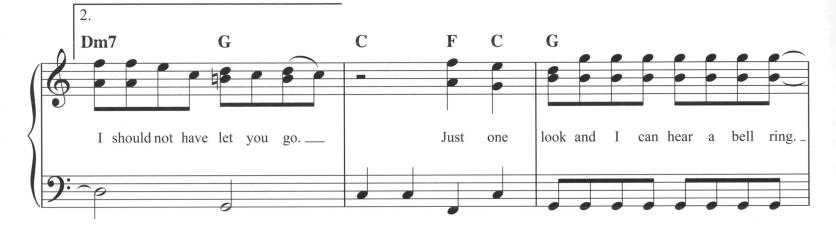

2.

Dm7　　　　G　　　　　C　　　F　　C　　G

I should not have let you go. ___　　　Just one　look and I can hear a bell ring. ___

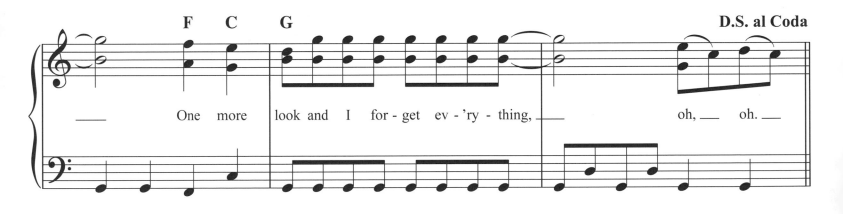

F　　C　　G　　　　　　　　　　　　　　　　D.S. al Coda

___ One more　look and I for - get ev - 'ry - thing, ___　　　oh, ___　oh. ___

CODA　F　　B♭　　F　　　　Dm7　　　　　G　　　　C

my,　　my,　　　　I should not have let you go. ___

SUPER TROUPER

Words and Music by BENNY ANDERSSON
and BJÖRN ULVAEUS

Su - per Trou - per beams are gon - na blind __ me but I won't feel

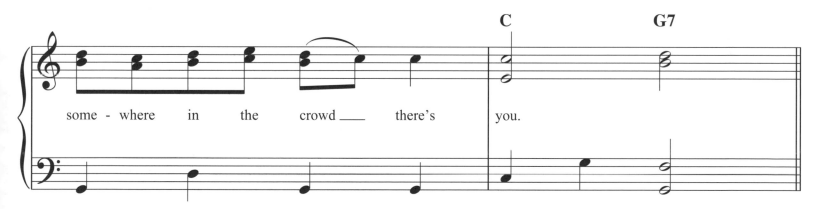

blue like I al - ways do, _____ 'cause

some - where in the crowd __ there's you.

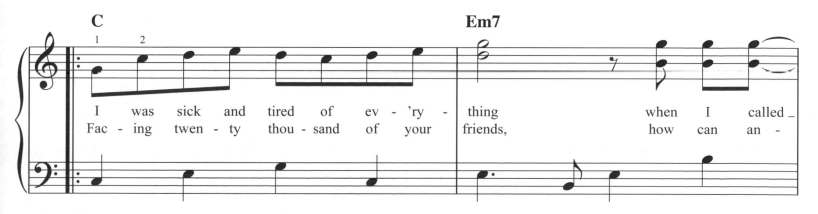

I was sick and tired of ev - 'ry - thing when I called __
Fac - ing twen - ty thou - sand of your friends, how can an -

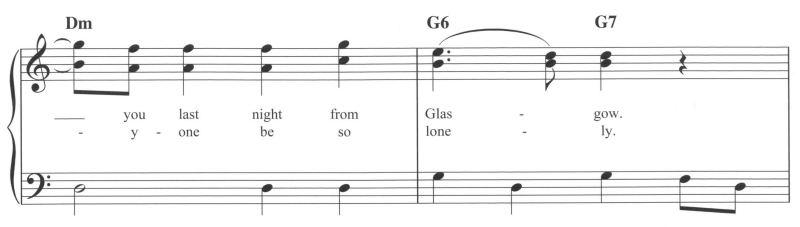

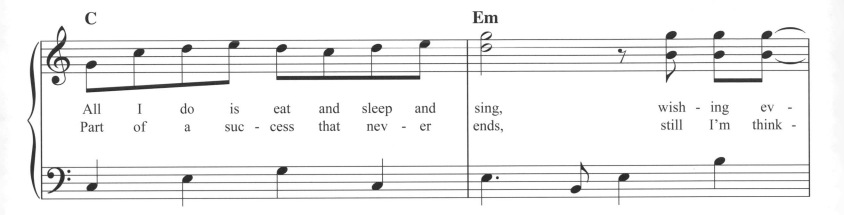

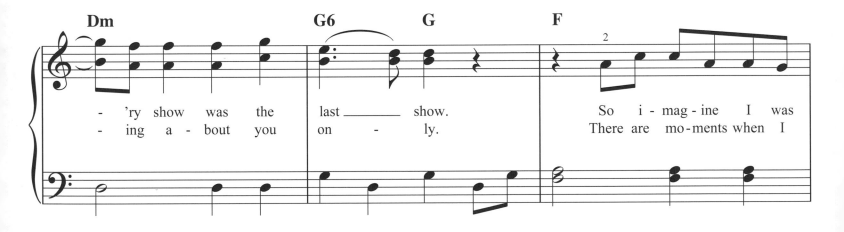

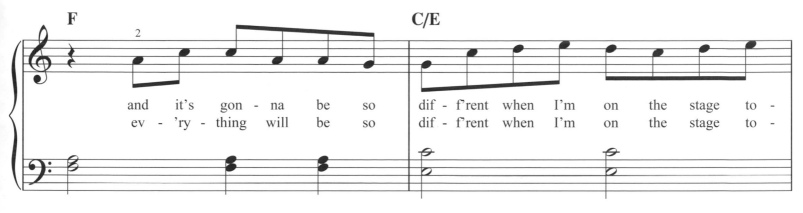

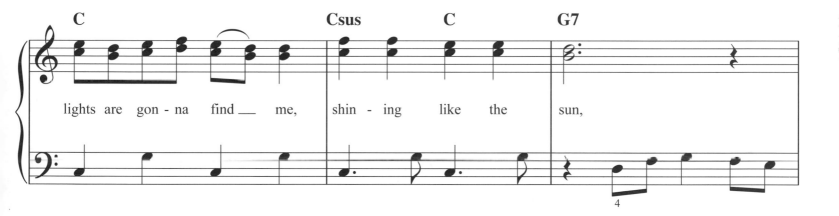

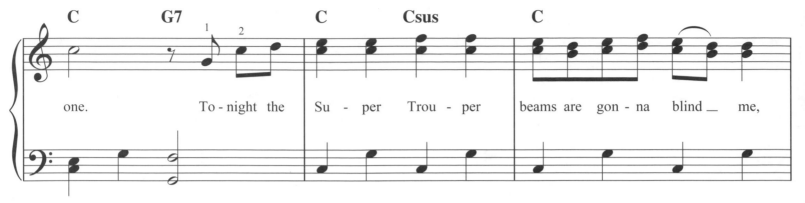

C   **G7**   **C**   **Csus**   **C**

one.   To - night the   Su - per Trou - per   beams are gon - na blind __ me,

To Coda ⊕

Csus   **C**   **G7**   **Dm7**

but I won't feel   blue   like I al - ways

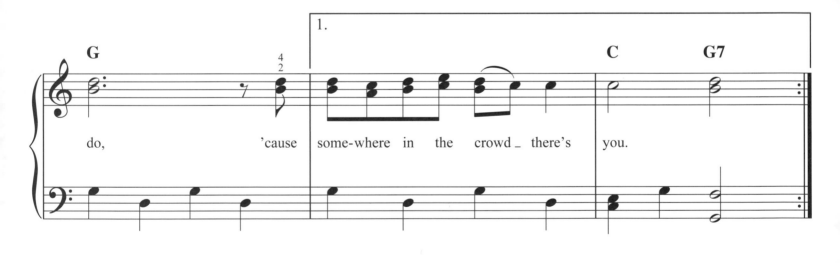

G   **1.**   **C**   **G7**

do,   'cause some-where in the crowd __ there's   you.

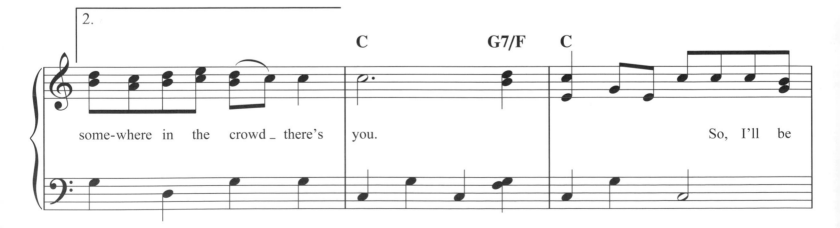

2.   **C**   **G7/F** **C**

some-where in the crowd __ there's you.   So, I'll be

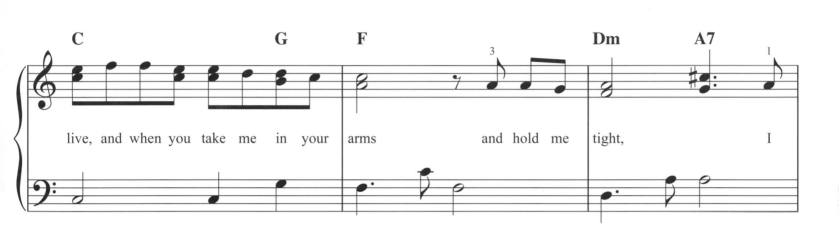

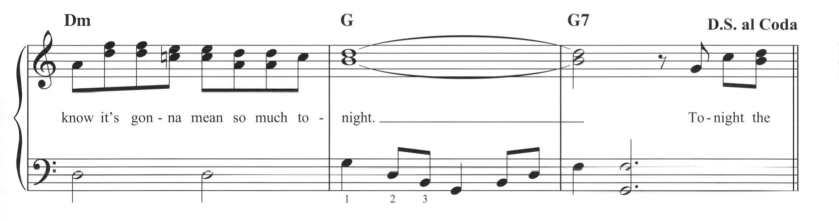

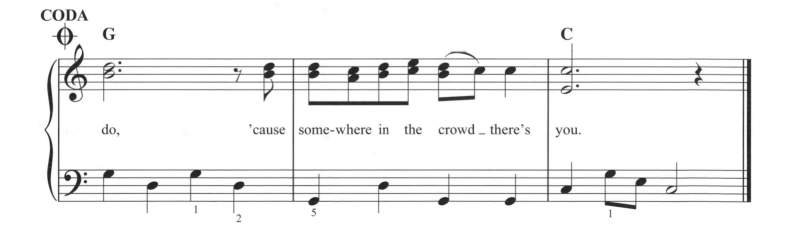

MY LOVE, MY LIFE

Words and Music by BENNY ANDERSSON
and BJÖRN ULVAEUS

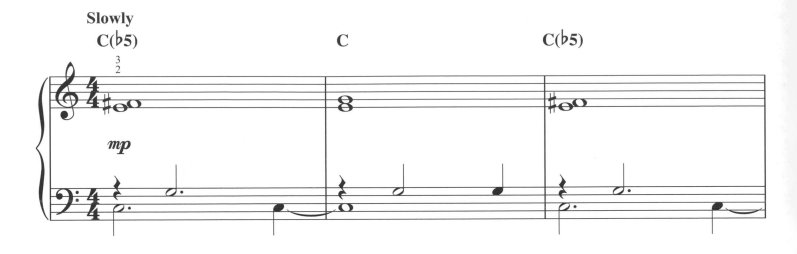

I've never felt this strong.
I held you close to me,

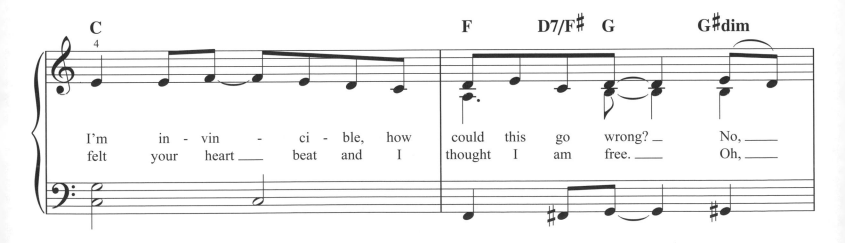

I'm in-vin-ci-ble, how could this go wrong? No,
felt your heart beat and I thought I am free. Oh,

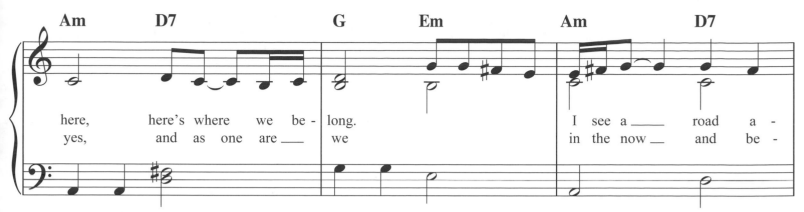

here, here's where we be - long.
yes, and as one are ___ we

I see a ___ road a -
in the now ___ and be -

head
yond,

I nev - er ___ thought ___ I would
noth - ing and ___ no one can ___

dare to
break this

tread.
bond.

mf Like an im - age pass - ing

by, my love, my life in the mir - or of your eyes. My love, ___ my

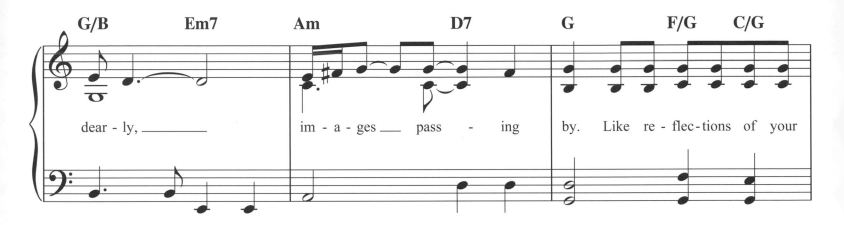

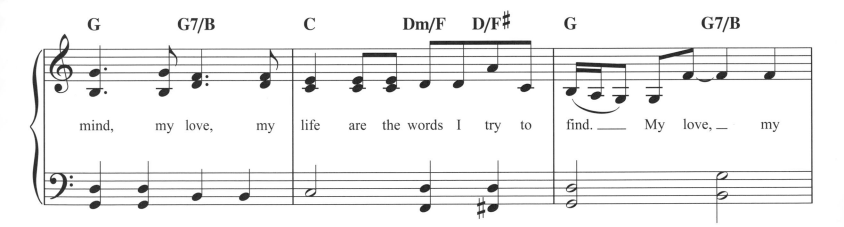

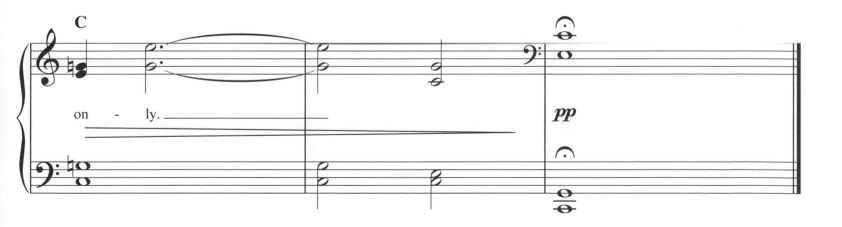

THE NAME OF THE GAME

Words and Music by BENNY ANDERSSON,
BJÖRN ULVAEUS and STIG ANDERSON

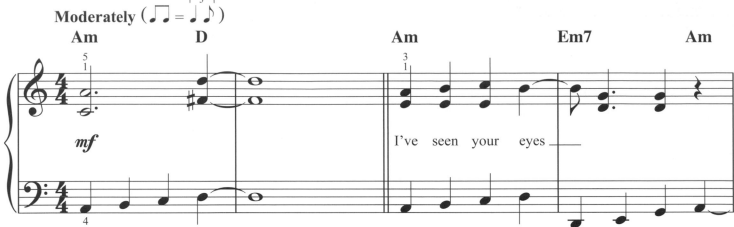

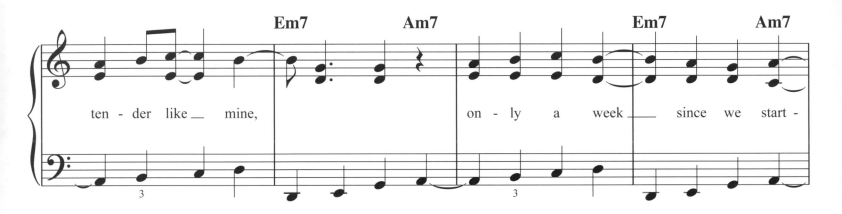

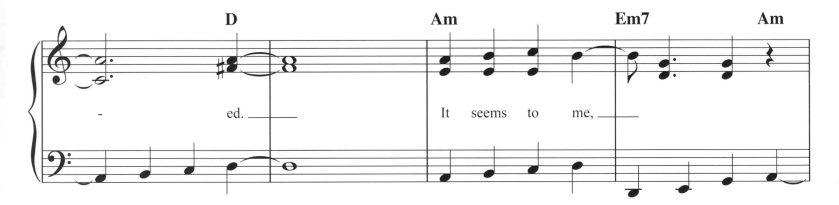

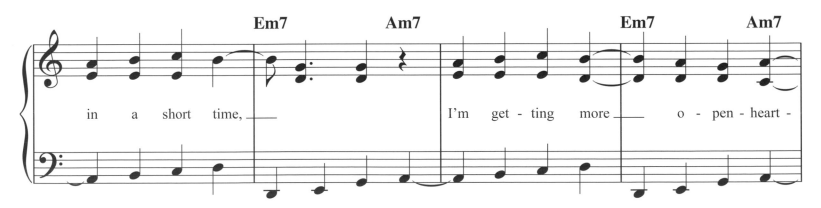

-ed. I was an im-pos-si-ble case,

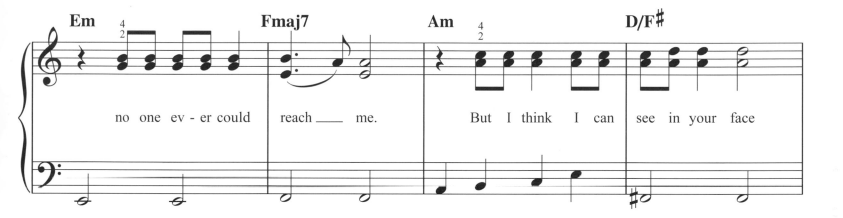

no one ev-er could reach me. But I think I can see in your face

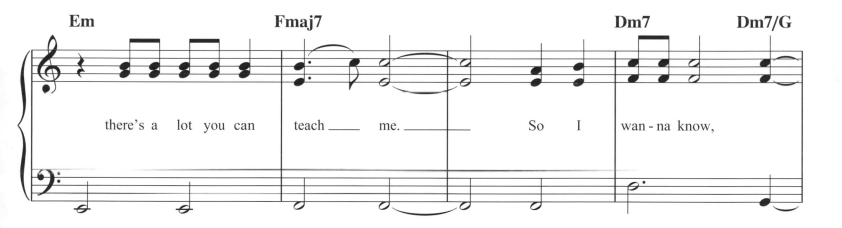

there's a lot you can teach me. So I wan-na know,

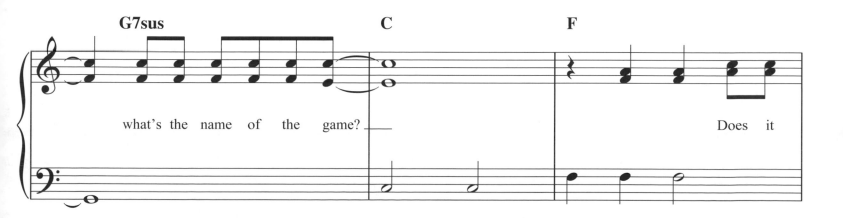

what's the name of the game? Does it

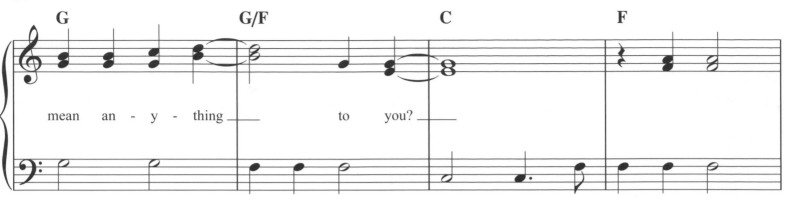

mean an-y-thing ____ to you? ____

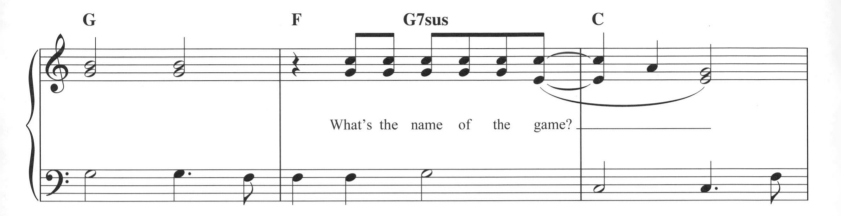

What's the name of the game? ____

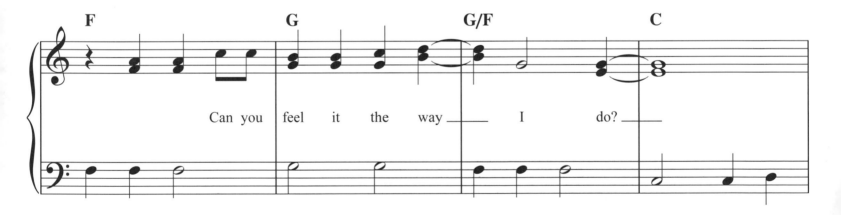

Can you feel it the way ____ I do? ____

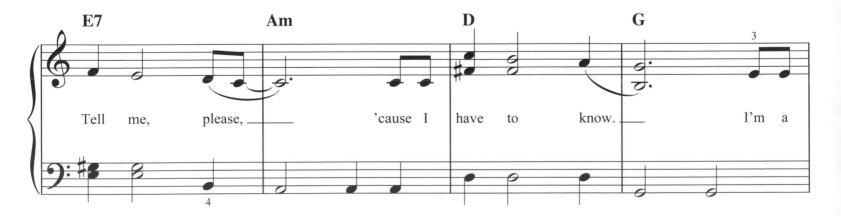

Tell me, please, ____ 'cause I have to know. ____ I'm a

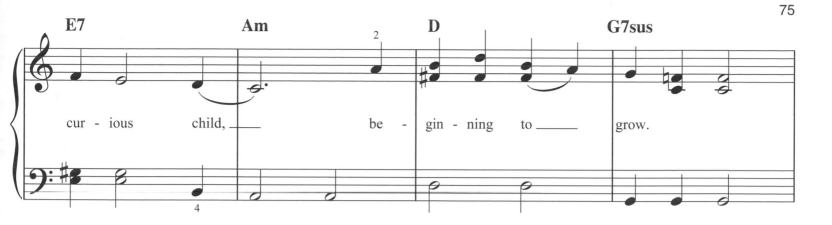

cur - ious child, ____ be - gin - ning to ____ grow.

And you make me talk. And you make me feel.

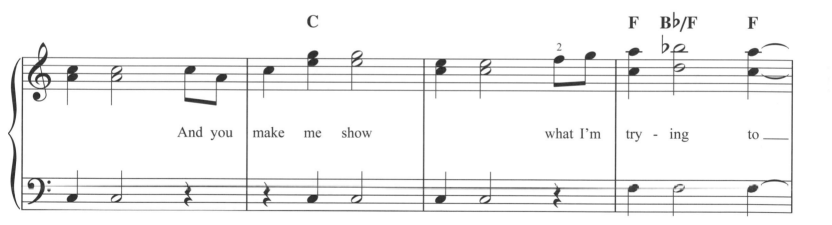

And you make me show what I'm try - ing to ____

____ con - ceal. If I trust in you, ____ will you let me down? __

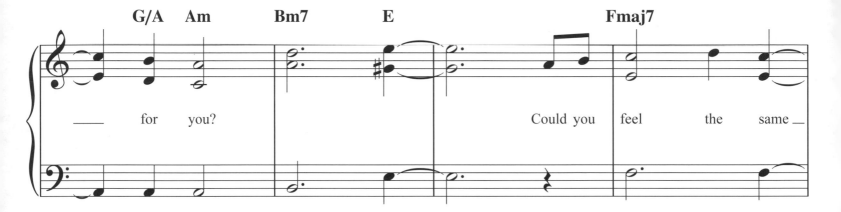

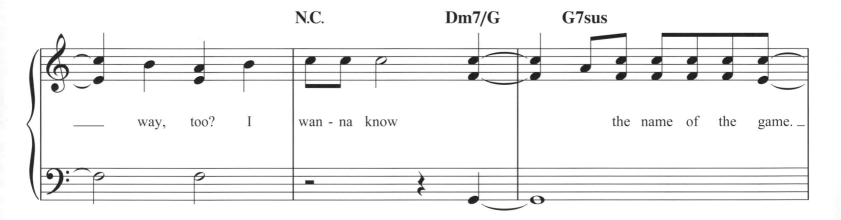

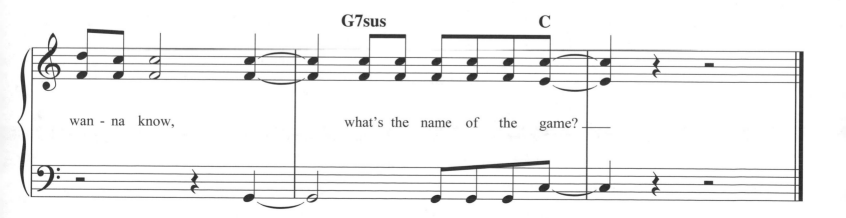

ONE OF US

Words and Music by BENNY ANDERSSON
and BJÖRN ULVAEUS

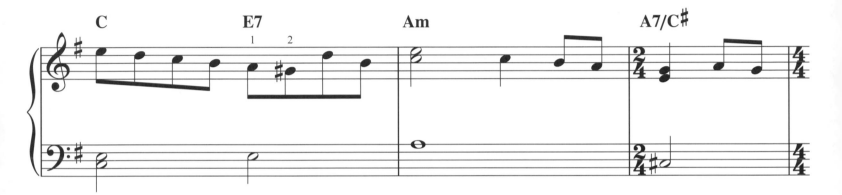

They pass me by,
I saw my-self
all of those great ro-manc-es.
as a con-cealed at-trac-tion.

C   Bm   Cmaj9   C   Dsus   D

It's as if you're rob - bing me ___ of my right - ful chanc - es.
I felt you kept me a - way ___ from the heat and the ac - tion.

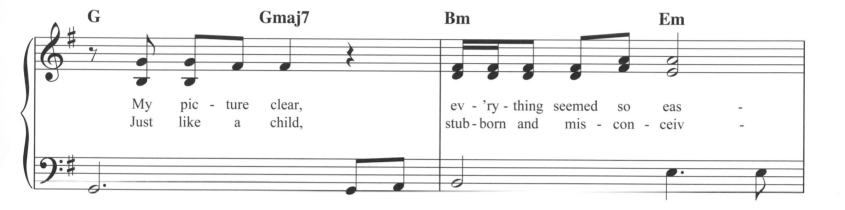

G   Gmaj7   Bm   Em

My pic - ture clear,   ev - 'ry - thing seemed so eas -
Just like a child,   stub - born and mis - con - ceiv -

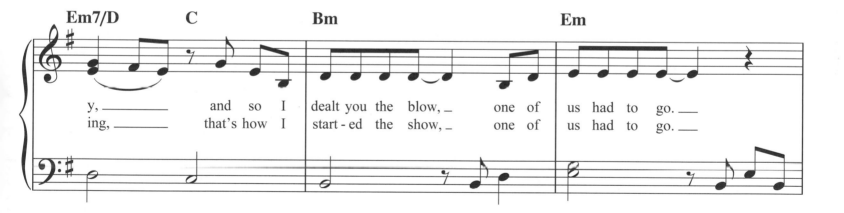

Em7/D   C   Bm   Em

y, ___ and so I dealt you the blow, _ one of us had to go. ___
ing, ___ that's how I start - ed the show, _ one of us had to go. ___

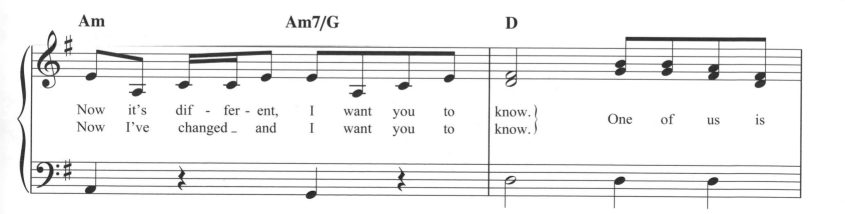

Am   Am7/G   D

Now it's dif - fer - ent, I want you to know. }
Now I've changed _ and I want you to know. }   One of us is

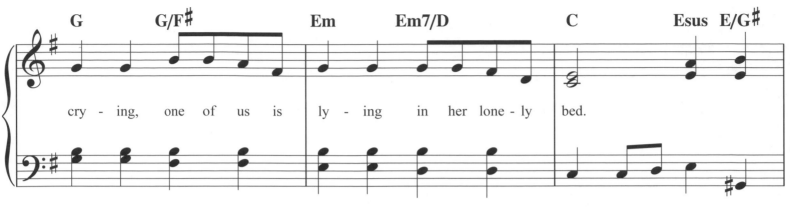

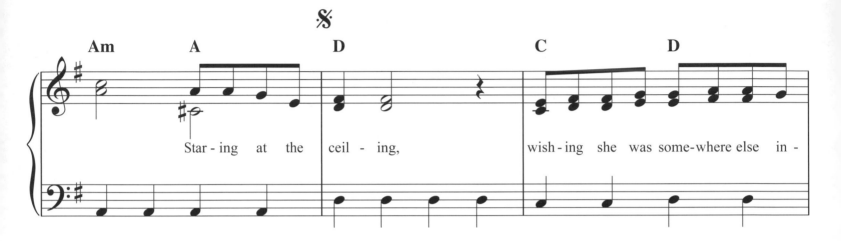

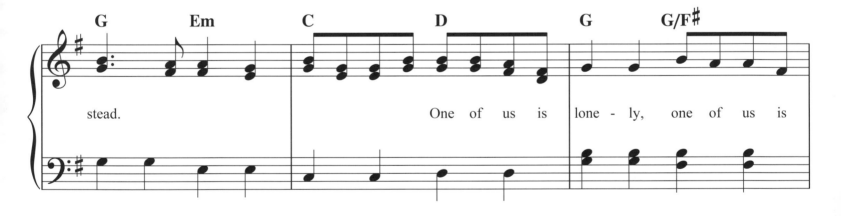

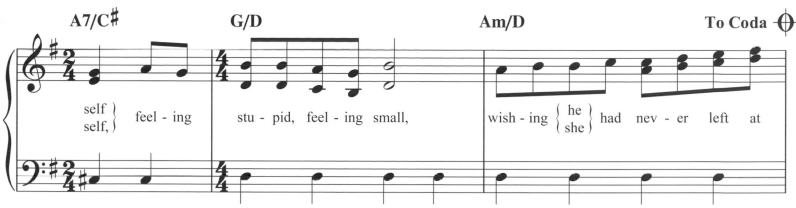

self } feel - ing stu - pid, feel - ing small,
self, } wish - ing { he } had nev - er left at
{ she }

1.
D
all.

2.
D
all. Nev - er left at all.

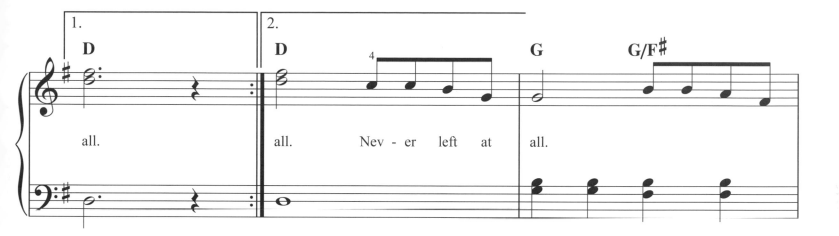

Em   Em7/D   C   E7   Am   A   D.S. al Coda

Star - ing at the

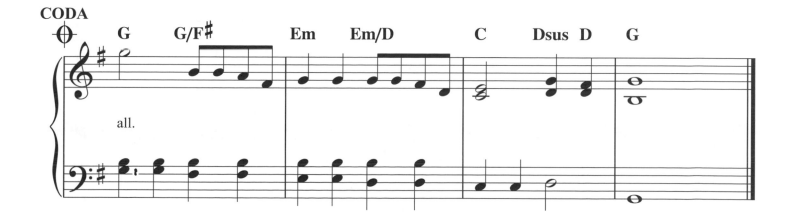

CODA
G   G/F♯   Em   Em/D   C   Dsus D   G
all.

WATERLOO

Words and Music by BENNY ANDERSSON,
BJÖRN ULVAEUS and STIG ANDERSON

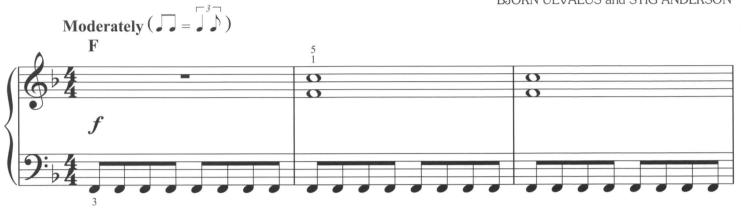

My, my, ____ at Wa - ter - loo ____ Na - po-
____ I tried ____ to hold ____ you back,

- le - on ____ did sur - ren - der. Oh yeah, ____ and I
____ but you ____ were strong - er. Oh yeah, ____ and now

____ have met ____ my des - ti - ny ____ in quite ____ a sim - 'lar
____ it seems ____ my on - ly chance is giv - in' up ____ the

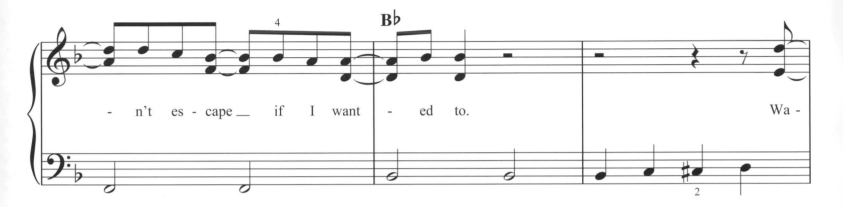

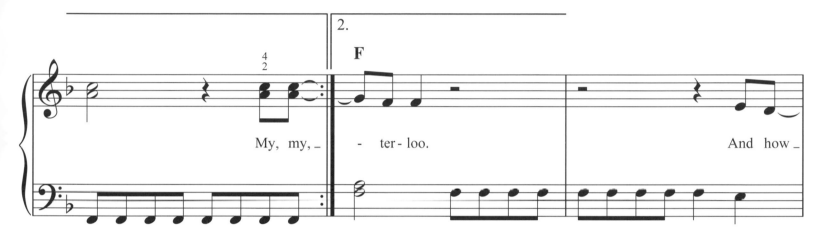

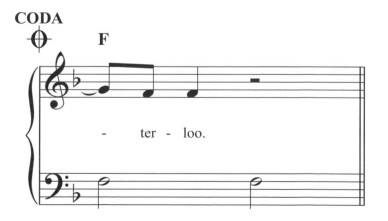

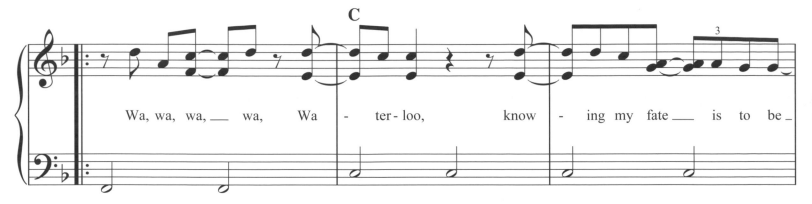

Wa, wa, wa, __ wa, Wa - ter - loo, know - ing my fate __ is to be __

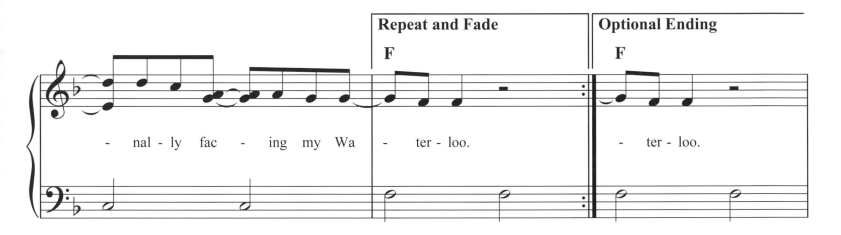

__ with you. Wa, __ wa, wa, wa, Wa - ter - loo, Fi -

Repeat and Fade   **Optional Ending**

- nal - ly fac - ing my Wa - ter - loo.   - ter - loo.

WHEN I KISSED THE TEACHER

Words and Music by BENNY ANDERSSON
and BJÖRN ULVAEUS

Moderately (in 2)

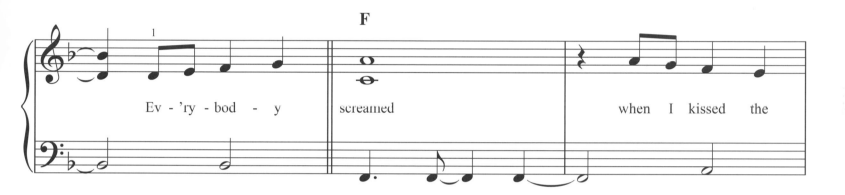

Ev - 'ry - bod - y   screamed   when I kissed the

teach - er,   and they must have   thought they dreamed _

when I kissed the   teach - er.   All my friends _ at

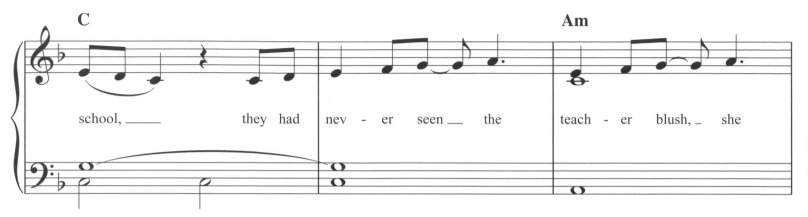

school, _____ they had nev - er seen __ the teach - er blush, _ she

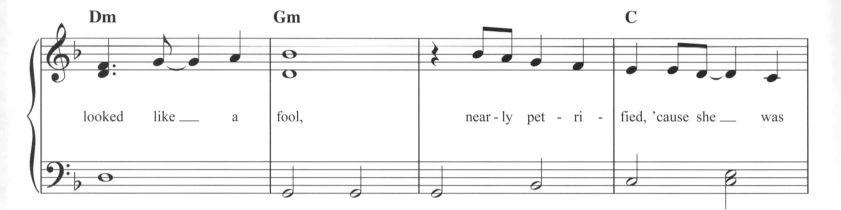

looked like __ a fool, near - ly pet - ri - fied, 'cause she __ was

tak - en by _____ sur - prise. | When I kissed the
trance | when I kissed the
day | when I kissed the

teach - er, could - n't quite be - lieve her eyes, _____
teach - er, sud - den - ly I took the chance, _
teach - er, all my sense had flown a - way, _____

89

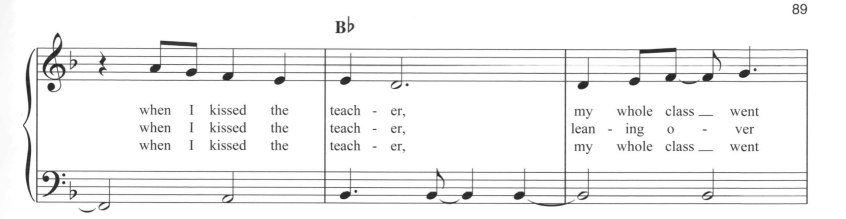

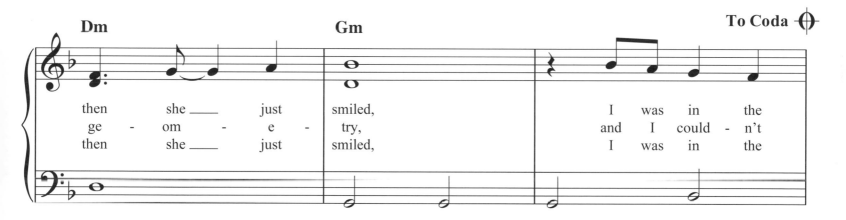

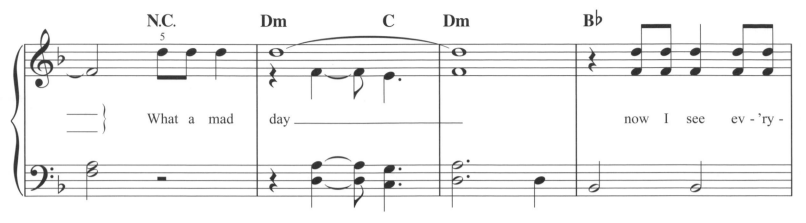

What a mad day _____ now I see ev -'ry -

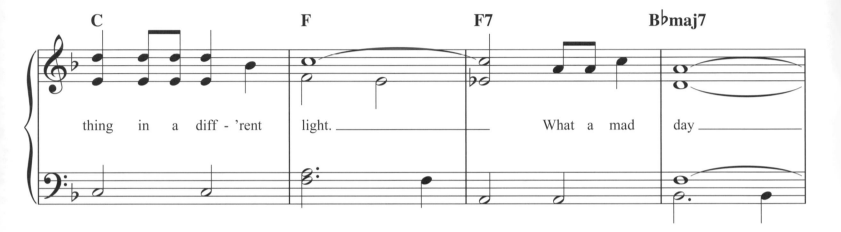

thing in a diff - 'rent light. _____ What a mad day _____

_____ I was up in teh air and she taught me a les - son al - right. _

I was in a   What a cra - zy

WHY DID IT HAVE TO BE ME?

Words and Music by BENNY ANDERSSON
and BJÖRN ULVAEUS

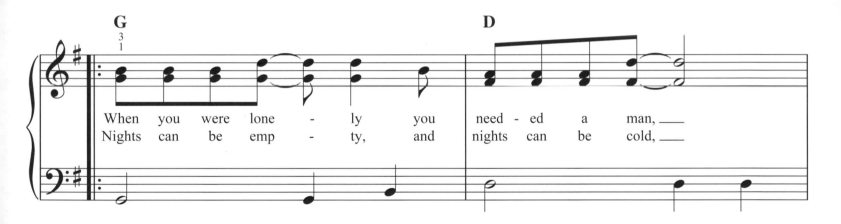

When you were lone - ly you | need - ed a man, ___

Nights can be emp - ty, and | nights can be cold, ___

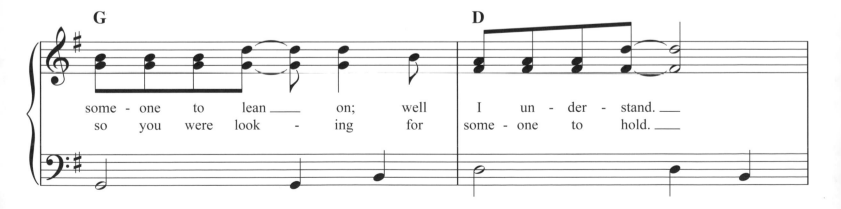

some - one to lean ___ on; well | I un - der - stand. ___

so you were look - ing well for | some - one to hold. ___

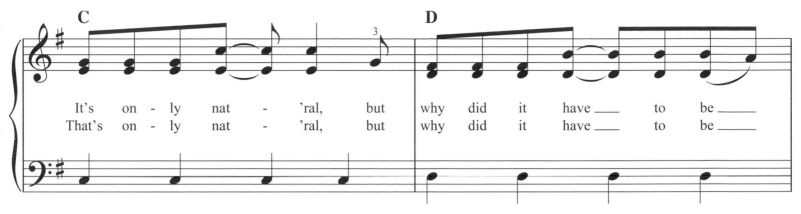

C / **D**

It's on - ly nat - 'ral, but why did it have ___ to be ___
That's on - ly nat - 'ral, but why did it have ___ to be ___

G / 1. / **D7** / 2. / **G7**

me?
me?

C / **G**

I was so lone - some; I was blue. ___ I could-n't help ___ it, it

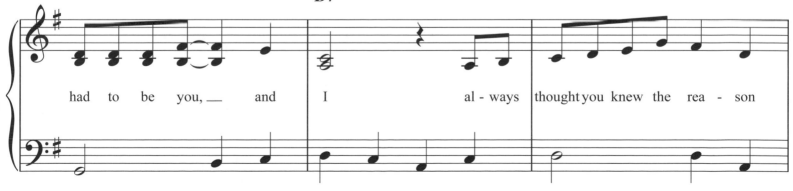

D7

had to be you, ___ and I al - ways thought you knew the rea - son

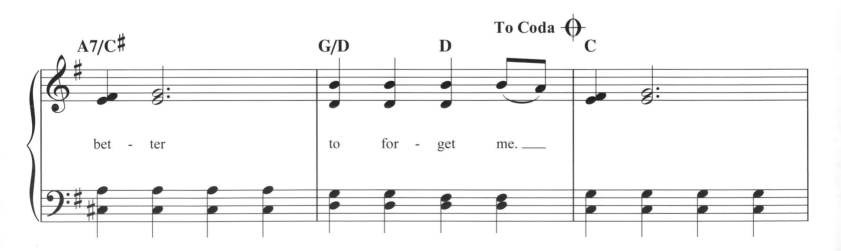

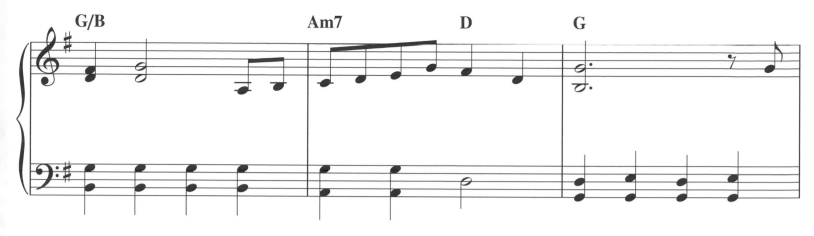

Men are the toys ____ in the

Fall - ing in love ____ with a

game that you play. ____

wom - an like you ____

When you are ti - red, you

hap - pens so quick - ly, there's

throw them a - way. ____

noth - ing to do. ____

That's on - ly nat - 'ral, but

It's on - ly nat - 'ral, but

why did it have __ to be __ me?
why did it have __ to be __ me?

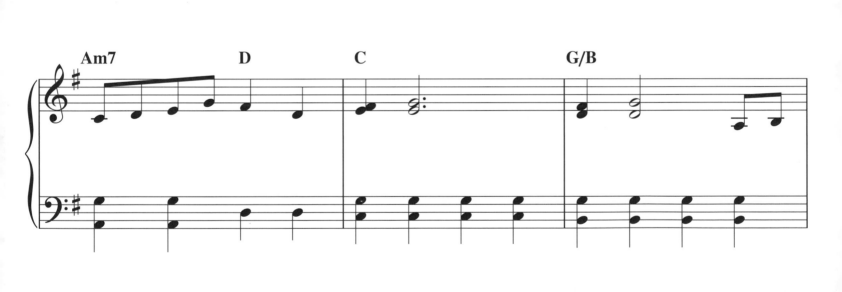